wheat gluten & dairy free

wheat
gluten &
dairy free

This edition published in 2011
LOVE FOOD is an imprint of Parragon Books Ltd

Parragon
Queen Street House
4 Queen Street
Bath BA1 1HE, UK

www.parragon.com

ISBN: 978-1-4454-6261-5

Printed in China

Additional photography by Clive Streeter
Food styling by Teresa Goldfinch
Additional recipes and introduction written by Christine France

Notes for the Reader
This book uses both metric and imperial measurements. Follow the same units of measurement throughout; do not mix metric and imperial. All spoon measurements are level: teaspoons are assumed to be 5 ml, and tablespoons are assumed to be 15 ml. Unless otherwise stated, milk is assumed to be full fat, eggs and individual vegetables are medium, and pepper is freshly ground black pepper.

The times given are an approximate guide only. Preparation times differ according to the techniques used by different people and the cooking times may also vary from those given. Optional ingredients, variations or serving suggestions have not been included in the calculations.

Recipes using raw or very lightly cooked eggs should be avoided by infants, the elderly, pregnant women, convalescents and anyone suffering from an illness. Pregnant and breastfeeding women are advised to avoid eating peanuts and peanut products. Sufferers from nut allergies should be aware that some of the ready-made ingredients used in the recipes in this book may contain nuts. Always check the packaging before use.

The publisher has taken great care to select ingredients for the recipes used in this book that will not cause a problem for anyone who is sensitive to wheat, gluten or dairy. Always read labels carefully and, if necessary, check with the manufacturer.

The nutritional information is given per serving and does not include the 'to serve' suggestions. Readers are advised that the salt amounts shown per recipe do not take into account any salt which may be added to taste, or at the table. Any ingredients that do not contain a weight measurement are medium-sized.

Contents

	Introduction	6
1	Breakfasts & Brunches	8
2	Light Lunches	46
3	Main Meals	84
4	Desserts & Baking	122
	Index	160

Introduction

A diagnosis of food allergy or intolerance need not cause such drastic changes to your diet as you may imagine. You'll need to be more careful in selecting foods and study labels thoroughly, but this soon becomes second nature and you'll see the benefits of a healthier diet.

What is the difference between allergy and intolerance?
There is some confusion between food allergy and intolerance, so it's important to establish which applies to you before deciding on treatment.

A food allergy occurs when a food triggers the body's immune system to react adversely, usually within minutes and often with quite dramatic effects. Once the immune system has been primed to produce these abnormal antibodies, the symptoms may be amplified the next time, causing severe allergic reactions to develop even with slight exposure.

Most adverse reactions to foods are caused by intolerances. These occur when the body's digestive system is unable to digest foods properly, and the reactions are slower to develop and less severe. Our bodies usually adapt to cope with a wide variety of foods, but when under stress, or on antibiotics, intolerances may develop.

What is coeliac disease?
Coeliac disease is an auto-immune disease, which occurs when the body's immune system reacts abnormally to gluten and produces antibodies that attack its own tissues. This causes inflammation and damage to the lining of the small intestine, which reduces the body's ability to absorb nutrients, causing symptoms such as anaemia, osteoporosis, weight loss, painful abdominal bloating and severe tiredness.

A blood test and biopsy can diagnose coeliac disease, and a doctor or dietitian will advise on a strict gluten-free diet. Once foods containing gluten are removed from the diet, the damaged intestinal lining can recover and function properly, but coeliac disease is a lifetime condition so you will need to restrict your diet permanently.

What is wheat allergy or intolerance?
Wheat allergy or intolerance can cause varied symptoms, including sinusitis, asthma, itchy and sore eyes, earache, headaches, migraine, muscle pain, stomach cramps, skin rashes, mouth ulcers, coughing, tiredness, depression, bloating, flatulence and nausea. Diagnosis involves blood and skin tests, and an exclusion diet is usually recommended.

What is dairy allergy or intolerance?
A dairy sensitivity is caused by an inability to digest lactose, a natural sugar in milk, or by casein, a milk protein. It often starts in childhood, but children may grow out of it. Symptoms vary, but include asthma, eczema, sinus problems, bloating, stomach pain and digestive problems. Depending on the suspected cause, a blood, skin or ingestion test is used for diagnosis, and treatment is by exclusion diet.

How to avoid missing out on vital nutrients
It's important to consult a doctor before

restricting your diet, and it's vital to ensure that you get all the essential nutrients by eating a good balance of food types.

When excluding gluten in wheat and other grains, a lack of B vitamins, iron and zinc can be made up by eating a selection of wholegrains such as rice, nuts, seeds and pulses, eggs, seafood and offal. Soya products, avocadoes, dark green vegetables and vegetable oils also supply vitamin E.

Dairy produce is a good source of protein, calcium and vitamins A and B12, so a dairy-free diet should include green leafy vegetables, soya products, canned fish, pulses and cereals.

Wheat-, dairy-, gluten-free alternatives
Most supermarkets and health food shops stock a useful range of gluten-, wheat- and dairy-free alternatives for restricted diets.

Coeliacs and those with wheat sensitivity can eat many other grains, including all varieties and forms of rice, buckwheat, amaranth, millet, quinoa, tapioca, sago, corn and maize. If you're sensitive to wheat you can also eat oats, barley and rye.

Some coeliacs can tolerate moderate amounts of oats, but you should ensure they are from an uncontaminated source, as there can be cross-contamination with other grains during processing at the mill.

Gluten-free flour, made from blends of rice, potato, tapioca and buckwheat flours, is useful for home baking. Some self-raising blends have xanthan gum added for elasticity, to improve texture in cakes. Single-grain flours like corn, rice or gram flour can be used for thickening sauces, binding or coating. Gluten-free pasta, breads and crispbreads are also available.

Many dairy-free substitutes for milk and dairy products use soya, rice, nuts, quinoa, oats or coconut. Olive, sunflower, soya, nut and vegetable oils, and non-dairy spreads are useful for cooking and spreading. Most people with lactose sensitivity will also react to goat's and sheep's milk.

Foods to watch out for
Always read labels on commercially prepared foods, as a surprising number contain hidden wheat, gluten or dairy products or derivatives.

As well as ready meals, burgers and sausages, many sauces, soups, stock cubes, mustard, spices and some brands of baking powder may contain wheat. Crisps and oven chips may have a wheat-based coating. Coeliacs should also look out for malt (from barley), used as a flavouring and colouring, and in beer-making. Check for dairy-based ingredients in desserts, baked goods, chocolate, artificial sweeteners and even some vegetable oil spreads.

As always, before you start any new diet, consult your doctor first.

Breakfasts & Brunches

banana crêpes

serves 4

50 g/1¾ oz buckwheat flour

50 g/1¾ oz gluten-free plain flour

pinch of salt

1 large egg, lightly beaten

125 ml/4 fl oz dairy-free milk

125 ml/4 fl oz water

40 g/1½ oz dairy-free spread

maple syrup bananas

40 g/1½ oz dairy-free spread

2 tbsp maple syrup

2 bananas, thickly sliced on the diagonal

Sift both types of flour and the salt into a mixing bowl. Make a well in the centre and add the beaten egg, milk and water. Using a balloon whisk, gradually mix the flour into the liquid ingredients, whisking well to get rid of any lumps, until you have a smooth batter.

Melt 25 g/1 oz of the spread in a small saucepan and stir it into the batter. Pour the batter into a jug, cover and leave to rest for 30 minutes.

Melt half the remaining spread in a medium-sized frying pan. When the pan is hot, pour in enough batter to make a thin crêpe, swirling the pan to achieve an even layer.

Cook one side until lightly browned, then, using a palette knife, turn over and cook the other side. Slide onto a warm plate and cover with foil while you cook the remaining crêpes, adding more spread when needed.

To make the maple syrup bananas, wipe the frying pan, add the spread and heat until melted. Stir in the maple syrup, then add the bananas and cook for 2–3 minutes, or until the bananas have just softened and the sauce has thickened and caramelized. To serve, fold the crêpes in half and half again, then top with the bananas.

Energy (kcals): 363   Fat (of which saturated fat): 20 g (4 g)   Carbohydrate (of which sugar): 41 g (19 g)   Salt: 0.7 g

apple granola

makes 10 portions

75 g/2¾ oz sunflower seeds

50 g/1¾ oz pumpkin seeds

90 g/3¼ oz shelled hazelnuts, roughly chopped

125 g/4½ oz buckwheat flakes

125 g/4½ oz rice flakes

125 g/4½ oz millet flakes

115 g/4 oz no-soak dried apple, roughly chopped

115 g/4 oz dried stoned dates, roughly chopped

Heat a dry frying pan over a medium heat, add the seeds and hazelnuts and lightly toast, shaking the pan frequently, for 4 minutes, or until golden brown. Transfer to a large mixing bowl and leave to cool.

Add the flakes, apple and dates to the bowl and mix thoroughly until combined. Store the muesli in an airtight jar or container.

Energy (kcals): 322   Fat (of which saturated fat): 12 g (1.5 g)   Carbohydrate (of which sugar): 44 g (14.5 g)   Salt: Trace

millet porridge

serves 4

225 g/8 oz millet flakes

450 ml/16 fl oz dairy-free milk

pinch of salt

freshly grated nutmeg

apricot purée

115 g/4 oz no-soak dried apricots, roughly chopped

300 ml/10 fl oz water

To make the apricot purée, put the apricots into a saucepan and cover with the water. Bring to the boil, then reduce the heat and simmer, half covered, for 20 minutes until the apricots are very tender. Transfer the apricots, along with any water left in the saucepan, to a food processor or blender and process until smooth. Set aside.

To make the porridge, put the millet flakes into a saucepan and add the milk and salt. Bring to the boil, then reduce the heat and simmer for 5 minutes, stirring frequently, until cooked and creamy.

To serve, spoon into four bowls and top with the apricot purée and a little nutmeg.

Energy (kcals): 289   Fat (of which saturated fat): 3 g (1 g)   Carbohydrate (of which sugar): 52 g (12 g)   Salt: 0.6 g

berry crunch

serves 4

75 g/2¾ oz rice, buckwheat or millet flakes, or a mixture

4 tbsp clear honey

500 g/1 lb 2 oz thick natural soya yogurt or dairy-free alternative

finely grated rind of 1 orange

225 g/8 oz frozen mixed berries, partially thawed, plus extra to decorate

Heat a dry frying pan over a medium heat, add the flakes and toast, shaking the pan, for 1 minute. Add half the honey and stir to coat the flakes. Cook, stirring constantly, until the flakes turn golden brown and slightly crisp.

Put the yogurt into a bowl and stir in the remaining honey and the orange rind. Gently stir in the berries, reserving a few to decorate. Leave for 10–15 minutes for the berries to release their juices, then stir again to give a swirl of colour.

To serve, spoon a layer of flakes into the bottom of four glasses, then top with a layer of the berry yogurt. Sprinkle with another layer of flakes and add another layer of the yogurt. Decorate with the reserved berries.

Energy (kcals): 225   Fat (of which saturated fat): 4 g (2.5 g)   Carbohydrate (of which sugar): 37 g (23 g)   Salt: 0.3 g

peachy tofu fool

serves 4

4 peaches or nectarines, stoned

3 tbsp orange juice

350 g/12 oz pack soft silken tofu, drained

2 tbsp maple syrup

40 g/1½ oz walnut pieces, roughly chopped

1 tbsp Demerara sugar

Roughly chop the peaches and purée with a hand blender or in a food processor until smooth. Add the orange juice and blend again.

Whizz the tofu with a hand blender or in a food processor until smooth. Stir in the maple syrup.

Place alternate tablespoonfuls of the fruit purée and tofu mixture into four tall stemmed glasses, or individual dishes, swirling lightly for a marbled effect.

Mix together the walnuts and Demerara, and spoon on top of the fools just before serving.

Energy (kcals): 252   Fat (of which saturated fat): 12 g (1.5 g)   Carbohydrate (of which sugar): 17.5 g (16 g)   Salt: Trace

banana smoothie

serves 4

125 g/4½ oz whole blanched almonds

600 ml/1 pint dairy-free milk

2 ripe bananas, halved

1 tsp natural vanilla extract

ground cinnamon, for sprinkling

Put the almonds into a food processor and process until very finely chopped. Add the milk, bananas and vanilla extract and blend until smooth and creamy.

Pour into glasses and sprinkle with cinnamon.

Energy (kcals): 287   Fat (of which saturated fat): 20 g (1.5 g)   Carbohydrate (of which sugar): 15 g (11 g)   Salt: Trace

strawberry shake

serves 4

200 g/7 oz strawberries, hulled

200 g/7 oz seedless green grapes, stems removed

175 ml/6 fl oz unsweetened soya milk

2 tbsp almond butter, or peanut butter

1 tbsp clear honey

4 whole strawberries, to decorate

1 tbsp sesame seeds

Place the strawberries, grapes, milk, almond butter and honey in a food processor or blender and process until smooth.

Half-dip the whole strawberries into the shake mixture, then dip into the sesame seeds.

Pour the shake into four glasses and top each with a sesame-dipped strawberry to serve.

Energy (kcals): 140   Fat (of which saturated fat): 7 g (1.5 g)   Carbohydrate (of which sugar): 15 g (15 g)   Salt: Trace

blueberry bars

makes 12

sunflower oil, for greasing

85 g/3 oz gluten-free
self-raising flour

55 g/2 oz quinoa flakes

55 g/2 oz puffed rice

55 g/2 oz flaked almonds

225 g/8 oz blueberries

100 g/3½ oz dairy-free
soya spread

100 g/3½ oz honey

1 egg, beaten

Preheat the oven to 180°C/350°F/Gas Mark 4. Grease a 28 x 18-cm/11 x 7-inch traybake tin and line the base with non-stick baking paper.

Mix together the flour, quinoa, puffed rice, almonds and blueberries. Place the soya spread and honey in a pan and heat gently until just melted, then stir evenly into the dry ingredients with the egg.

Spread the mixture into the prepared tin, smoothing with a palette knife. Bake in the oven for 25–30 minutes, until golden brown and firm.

Leave to cool in the tin for 15 minutes, and cut into 12 bars. Transfer to a wire rack to continue cooling.

Energy (kcals): 277   Fat (of which saturated fat): 13 g (2.5 g)   Carbohydrate (of which sugar): 21 g (10 g)   Salt: 0.3 g

plum pancakes

serves 6

8 red plums, stoned and
cut into quarters

100 ml/3½ fl oz
maple syrup

1 tbsp lemon juice

1 piece star anise

200 g/7 oz gluten-free
and wheat-free plain
flour blend

1½ tsp gluten-free
baking powder

2 eggs, beaten

200 ml/7 fl oz sweetened
soya milk

100 g/3½ oz plain
soya yogurt

1 tbsp sunflower oil,
plus extra for greasing

Place the plums, syrup, lemon juice and star anise in a pan and heat until almost boiling. Reduce the heat, cover and cook gently for 8–10 minutes, stirring occasionally, until tender.

Place the flour, baking powder, eggs, milk, yogurt and oil in a blender or food processor and blend to a smooth, bubbly batter.

Lightly grease a large, heavy-based frying pan or griddle pan and heat until very hot. Drop tablespoonfuls of the batter onto the pan and cook for 5–6 minutes, turning once, until golden and set. Cook in batches to make about 24 pancakes.

To serve, stack 4 pancakes on each plate and spoon over the plums and juices.

Energy (kcals): 266   Fat (of which saturated fat): 8 g (1.5 g)   Carbohydrate (of which sugar): 42.5 g (16.5 g)   Salt: 0.6 g

potato cakes

serves 4

115 g/4 oz cold
mashed potatoes

200 ml/7 fl oz
dairy-free milk

75 g/2¾ oz gluten-free
self-raising flour

pinch of salt

1 egg, beaten

sunflower oil, for frying

to serve

8 good-quality bacon
rashers, grilled
until crisp

1½ tbsp maple syrup

Put the mashed potatoes and milk into a food processor or blender and process to a thin purée.

Sift the flour and salt into a mixing bowl, make a well in the centre of the flour and add the beaten egg and potato purée. Using a balloon whisk, gradually mix the flour into the liquid ingredients, whisking well to make a smooth, creamy, fairly thick batter.

Heat a little oil in a large, non-stick frying pan. Pour a tablespoonful of batter per cake into the pan – you will probably fit about 3 in the pan at one time. Cook each cake for 2 minutes on each side until golden brown. Remove from the pan and keep warm while you cook the remaining potato cakes.

Divide the cakes between 4 warmed plates, top each serving with 2 bacon rashers and drizzle with maple syrup.

Energy (kcals): 276   Fat (of which saturated fat): 15 g (4 g)   Carbohydrate (of which sugar): 21.5 g (4 g)   Salt: 2.3 g

chickpea fritters

serves 4

125 g/4½ oz gluten-free
self-raising flour

1 egg, beaten

175 ml/6 fl oz unsweetened
soya milk

140 g/5 oz spring onions,
thinly sliced

400 g/14 oz canned
chickpeas, drained

4 tbsp chopped coriander

sunflower oil, for frying

salt and pepper

coriander sprigs, to garnish

Sift the flour into a bowl and make a well in the centre. Add the egg and milk and stir into the flour, then whisk to make a smooth batter.

Stir in the onions, chickpeas and coriander, then season well with salt and pepper.

Heat the oil in a large, heavy-based frying pan and add tablespoonfuls of the batter. Fry in batches for 4–5 minutes, turning once, until golden brown.

Serve the fritters stacked on warmed serving plates, garnished with coriander sprigs.

Energy (kcals): 250   Fat (of which saturated fat): 6 g (0.8 g)   Carbohydrate (of which sugar): 36 g (4 g)   Salt: 0.3 g

sausage brunch

serves 4

4 gluten-free sausages or vegetarian alternative

sunflower oil, for frying

4 boiled potatoes, cooled and diced

8 cherry tomatoes

4 eggs, beaten

salt and pepper

Preheat the grill to medium–high. Arrange the sausages on a foil-lined grill pan and cook under the preheated grill, turning occasionally, for 12–15 minutes, or until cooked through and golden brown. Leave to cool slightly, then slice into bite-sized pieces.

Meanwhile, heat a little oil in a medium-sized (25-cm/10-inch), heavy-based frying pan with a heatproof handle over a medium heat. Add the potatoes and cook until golden brown and crisp all over, then add the tomatoes and cook for a further 2 minutes. Arrange the sausages in the pan so that there is an even distribution of potatoes, tomatoes and sausages.

Add a little more oil to the pan if it seems dry. Season the beaten eggs to taste and pour the mixture over the ingredients in the pan. Cook for 3 minutes, without stirring or disturbing the eggs. Place the pan under the preheated grill for 3 minutes, or until the top is just cooked. Cut into wedges to serve.

Energy (kcals): 137   Fat (of which saturated fat): 6.5 g (2 g)   Carbohydrate (of which sugar): 13 g (3 g)   Salt: 0.5 g

mushroom röstis

serves 4

300 g/10½ oz celeriac, peeled

1 small onion

3 tbsp chopped fresh parsley

4 portobello mushrooms (about 100 g/3½ oz)

4 tbsp olive oil

4 eggs

2 tbsp unsweetened soya milk

salt and pepper

Preheat the oven to 200°C/400°F/Gas Mark 6. Coarsely grate the celeriac and onion in a food processor or by hand. Add 2 tablespoons of the parsley and season well.

Place the mushrooms on a baking sheet, brush with about 1 tablespoon of oil and season with salt and pepper. Bake for 10–12 minutes.

Heat 2 tablespoons of the oil in a large, heavy-based frying pan. Place four large spoonfuls of the celeriac mixture in the pan, pressing with a palette knife to flatten. Fry for about 10 minutes, turning once, until golden. Drain on kitchen paper and keep hot.

Meanwhile, beat the eggs with the milk, remaining parsley and salt and pepper. Heat the remaining oil in a small pan and cook the egg, stirring, until just set.

Place the röstis on warmed serving plates, top each with a mushroom and spoon over the scrambled eggs.

Energy (kcals): 213   Fat (of which saturated fat): 18 g (3.4 g)   Carbohydrate (of which sugar): 3.5 g (2.5 g)   Salt: 0.4 g

chive cornbread

serves 4

4 tbsp olive oil,
plus extra for greasing

125 g/4½ oz medium
cornmeal

100 g/3½ oz soya flour

1 tbsp gluten-free baking
powder

15 g/½ oz chopped chives

1 large egg, beaten

300 ml/10 fl oz
unsweetened soya milk

8 pancetta slices

1 ripe avocado

salt and pepper

Preheat the oven to 190°C/375°F/Gas Mark 5. Grease an 18-cm/7-inch square shallow cake tin with oil.

Sift the cornmeal, flour, baking powder and salt and pepper into a bowl. Stir in the chives.

Beat together the egg, milk and oil and stir into the dry ingredients, mixing evenly. Spoon the mixture into the tin and smooth the top with a palette knife.

Bake for 30–35 minutes, or until firm and golden. Meanwhile, place the pancetta slices on a baking sheet and bake for 10–12 minutes, until golden and crisp. Drain on kitchen paper.

Halve, stone and slice the avocado. Cut the cornbread into four squares and serve warm, topped with pancetta and avocado.

Energy (kcals): 590   Fat (of which saturated fat): 39 g (8.5 g)   Carbohydrate (of which sugar): 30 g (3.5 g)   Salt: 2.8 g

broccoli hash

serves 4

400 g/14 oz floury potatoes
(e.g. Maris Piper) cut into
1-cm/½-inch cubes

175 g/6 oz broccoli,
cut into small florets

2 tbsp sunflower oil

1 onion, finely chopped

1 large red pepper,
cut into small dice

¼–½ tsp dried chilli flakes

4 large eggs

salt and pepper

Cook the potatoes in lightly salted boiling water for 6 minutes. Drain well. Blanch or steam the broccoli for 3 minutes.

Heat the oil in a large frying pan over a fairly high heat, add the onion and red pepper and fry for 2–3 minutes to soften. Add the potatoes and cook, turning occasionally, for 6–8 minutes, until tender.

Stir in the broccoli and chilli flakes then leave over a low heat, turning the mixture occasionally until golden brown. Season to taste.

Meanwhile, bring a wide pan of water to just simmering point. Break the eggs into the water and poach gently for 3–4 minutes, until softly set.

Spoon the hash onto warmed plates and top each portion with a poached egg.

Energy (kcals): 260   Fat (of which saturated fat): 13.9 g (2.8 g)   Carbohydrate (of which sugar): 20.9 g (4.7 g)   Salt: 0.27 g

vegetable pho

serves 4

1.5 litres/2¾ pints gluten-free vegetable stock

2 tbsp gluten-free tamari

2 garlic cloves, thinly sliced

2.5-cm/1-inch piece ginger, thinly sliced

1 cinnamon stick

1 bay leaf

1 medium carrot, thinly shredded

1 small fennel bulb, thinly sliced

150 g/5½ oz vermicelli rice noodles

85 g/3 oz button mushrooms, sliced

115 g/4 oz beansprouts

4 spring onions, thinly sliced diagonally

3 tbsp chopped coriander

small handful of basil leaves

chopped red chillies, lime wedges and gluten-free tamari, to serve

Place the stock in a large pan with the tamari, garlic, ginger, cinnamon and bay leaf. Bring to the boil, reduce the heat, cover and simmer for about 20 minutes.

Add the carrot and fennel and simmer for 1 minute. Add the noodles and simmer for a further 4 minutes.

Add the mushrooms, beansprouts and spring onions and return to the boil.

Ladle into soup bowls and sprinkle with coriander and basil leaves. Serve with chillies, lime wedges and tamari to season at the table.

Energy (kcals): 182   Fat (of which saturated fat): 1.2 g (0.1 g)   Carbohydrate (of which sugar): 32.8 g (3.8 g)   Salt: 1.4 g

fruit soda bread

makes 1 loaf (serves 6)

55 g/2 oz ready-to-eat
pitted prunes, chopped

55 g/2 oz ready-to-eat dried
apricots, chopped

40 g/1½ oz ready-to-eat
dried apples, chopped

40 g/1½ oz dried
cranberries

150 ml/5 fl oz apple juice

2 tbsp sunflower oil,
plus extra for greasing

450 g/1 lb gluten- and
wheat-free plain white
flour blend

1½ tbsp gluten-free
baking powder

2 tsp xanthan gum

¼ tsp salt

225 ml/8 fl oz soya milk,
plus extra for brushing

4 tbsp maple syrup

1 tbsp pumpkin seeds

Place the prunes, apricots, apples and cranberries in a bowl and pour over the apple juice. Cover and leave to stand for about 30 minutes.

Preheat the oven to 200°C/400°F/Gas Mark 6. Brush a baking sheet with oil. Sift the flour, baking powder, xanthan gum and salt into a bowl and make a well in the centre. Mix the oil, milk and maple syrup and add to the dry ingredients with the fruits and juice, mixing lightly to a soft, but not sticky, dough. Add a little more milk if the dough feels dry.

Shape the dough to a smooth round on the prepared baking sheet, flatten slightly and cut a deep cross through the centre almost to the base. Gently pull the wedges apart at the points. Brush with milk and sprinkle with pumpkin seeds.

Bake in the preheated oven for 25–30 minutes, or until golden brown and the base sounds hollow when tapped.

Energy (kcals): 427   Fat (of which saturated fat): 7 g (1 g)   Carbohydrate (of which sugar): 84 g (20 g)   Salt: 1.5 g

breakfast muffins

makes 12

300 g/10½ oz gluten-and wheat-free plain white flour blend

4 tsp gluten-free baking powder

½ tsp xanthan gum

1 tsp ground mixed spice

140 g/5 oz light muscovado sugar

40 g/1½ oz sunflower seeds

175 g/6 oz grated carrots

finely grated rind and juice 1 small orange

2 eggs, beaten

150 ml/5 fl oz unsweetened soya milk

100 ml/3½ fl oz sunflower oil

1 tsp vanilla extract

Preheat the oven to 200°C/400°F/Gas Mark 6. Place 12 paper muffin cases into a deep muffin tray.

Sift the flour, baking powder, xanthan gum and mixed spice into a large bowl. Stir in the sugar with 25 g/1 oz sunflower seeds, carrots and orange rind.

Lightly beat together the orange juice, eggs, milk, oil and vanilla with a fork and stir into the dry ingredients, mixing to make a rough batter.

Spoon the batter into the muffin cases and sprinkle with the remaining sunflower seeds. Bake in the oven for about 20 minutes, or until well risen and golden brown. Serve warm.

Energy (kcals): 231   Fat (of which saturated fat): 9.5 g (1.5 g)   Carbohydrate (of which sugar): 35 g (13 g)   Salt: 0.7 g

Light Lunches

potato salad

serves 6

500 g/1 lb 2 oz
new potatoes

16 vine-ripened cherry
tomatoes, halved

70 g/2½ oz black olives,
stoned and
coarsely chopped

4 spring onions, sliced

2 tbsp chopped fresh mint

2 tbsp chopped
fresh parsley

2 tbsp chopped
fresh coriander

juice of 1 lemon

3 tbsp extra virgin olive oil

salt and pepper

Cook the potatoes in a saucepan of lightly salted boiling water for 15 minutes, or until tender. Drain, then leave to cool slightly. Cut into halves or quarters, depending on the size of the potato. Then combine with the tomatoes, olives, spring onions and herbs in a salad bowl.

Mix the lemon juice and oil together in a small bowl or jug and pour over the potato salad. Season to taste with salt and pepper before serving.

Energy (kcals): 140   Fat (of which saturated fat): 8 g (1 g)   Carbohydrate (of which sugar): 15 g (3 g)   Salt: 0.2 g

onion soup

serves 4

800 g/1 lb 12 oz red onions, peeled and quartered

1 tbsp olive oil

15 g/½ oz dairy-free spread

250 ml/9 fl oz dry white wine

1.2 litres/2 pints gluten-free vegetable stock

1 fresh rosemary sprig, plus extra to garnish

1 tsp chopped fresh thyme

1 tsp Dijon mustard

salt and pepper

croûtons

300 ml/10 fl oz water

60 g/2½ oz fine instant polenta

½ tsp salt

1 tbsp chopped fresh rosemary

olive oil, for brushing

Preheat the oven to 200°C/400°F/Gas Mark 6. Put the onions and oil into a roasting tin and toss well. Dot with the spread, season to taste with salt and roast in the preheated oven for 45 minutes. Remove from the oven and leave to cool slightly.

Discard the outer layer of each onion segment if crisp, then cut the remainder into thick slices. Put the onions into a large, heavy-based saucepan with the wine and bring to the boil. Cook until most of the wine has evaporated. Stir in the stock and herbs and cook over a medium–low heat for 30–35 minutes, or until reduced and thickened. Stir in the mustard and season to taste with salt and pepper.

Meanwhile, to make the polenta croûtons, heat the water to boiling point in a saucepan. Pour in the polenta in a steady stream and cook, stirring constantly with a wooden spoon, for 5 minutes, or until thickened. Stir in the salt and rosemary. Cover a chopping board with a sheet of clingfilm, then, using a palette knife, spread out the polenta in an even layer about 1 cm/½ inch thick. Leave to cool and firm up. Cut into bite-sized cubes, brush with oil and arrange on a baking sheet. Cook in the oven, turning occasionally, for 10–15 minutes, or until crisp and lightly golden brown. Remove the rosemary from the soup and discard. Transfer half the soup to a food processor or blender and process until smooth, then return to the saucepan and stir well. To serve, ladle into 4 warmed bowls and top with the polenta croûtons and sprigs of rosemary.

Energy (kcals): 238   Fat (of which saturated fat): 7.4 g (1 g)   Carbohydrate (of which sugar): 25.4 g (11.1 g)   Salt: 0.68 g

golden pilaf

serves 4

450 ml/16 fl oz gluten-free vegetable or chicken stock

200 g/7 oz toasted buckwheat

3 tbsp olive oil

1 medium onion, sliced

2 garlic cloves, thinly sliced

2-cm/¾-inch piece ginger, thinly sliced

½ tsp ground turmeric

½ tsp ground cinnamon

4 tbsp orange juice

85 g/3 oz sultanas

2 medium carrots, coarsely grated

55 g/2 oz pine nuts, toasted

salt and pepper

shreds of orange zest and coriander, to garnish

Bring the stock to the boil and add the buckwheat. Simmer for 5–6 minutes until most of the liquid is absorbed, then add 1 tablespoon of the oil, cover and leave on a low heat for 10 minutes, until tender.

Heat the remaining oil and fry the onion on a medium heat for 5–6 minutes, stirring occasionally, until soft and golden brown.

Add the garlic and ginger and stir for 1 minute, then stir in the turmeric, cinnamon, orange juice and sultanas and cook for 1 minute.

Add the carrots, cooked buckwheat and pine nuts, stirring until evenly heated. Season to taste with salt and pepper.

Pile the pilaf onto a warm serving plate and scatter over the orange zest and coriander. Serve either on its own or as an accompaniment to grilled or roasted meats.

Energy (kcals): 446   Fat (of which saturated fat): 19 g (2 g)   Carbohydrate (of which sugar): 60 g (21 g)   Salt: 0.2 g

risotto cakes

serves 6

1 tbsp olive oil,
plus extra for greasing

200 g/7 oz arborio
risotto rice

500 ml/18 fl oz gluten-free
chicken or vegetable
stock

100 ml/3½ fl oz coconut
milk

8 spring onions,
thinly sliced

225 g/8 oz young spinach
leaves

2 eggs, beaten

2 tbsp chopped coriander

salt and pepper

mixed lettuce leaves,
to serve

Preheat the oven to 200°C/400°F/Gas Mark 6. Brush a 23-cm/ 9-inch cake tin with oil and line the base with non-stick paper.

Heat the oil in a large pan, add the rice and cook, stirring, for 1 minute. Add a ladleful of stock and cook, stirring often, until the liquid is almost absorbed. Continue to add the stock gradually until the rice is almost tender and there is no free liquid. Stir in the coconut milk and spring onions and season well. Remove from the heat.

Meanwhile, place the spinach in a pan and heat until the leaves are wilted. Drain, pressing out any free liquid. Stir into the rice with the beaten eggs and chopped coriander.

Tip the mixture into the prepared cake tin, smoothing the top, and bake for 25–30 minutes, until just set.

Turn out and serve hot or cold, cut into wedges, with the lettuce leaves.

Energy (kcals): 345   Fat (of which saturated fat): 14 g (6 g)   Carbohydrate (of which sugar): 41 g (2.5 g)   Salt: 0.3 g

bruschettas

serves 4

2 tbsp olive oil,
plus extra for brushing

500 ml/18 fl oz water

100 g/3½ oz instant
polenta

16 cherry vine tomatoes

salt and pepper

tapenade

25 g/1 oz sun-dried
tomatoes, soaked and
drained

55 g/2 oz pitted black olives

2 tbsp salted capers, rinsed

2 tbsp chopped flat-leaf
parsley

1 clove garlic, crushed

juice of ½ lemon

2 tbsp extra virgin olive oil

salt and pepper

Grease a 450-g/1-lb loaf tin with oil. Place the water in a large pan with a pinch of salt and bring to the boil.

Sprinkle in the polenta and stir constantly over moderate heat for about 5 minutes, until thick and smooth. Remove from the heat, stir in the oil and salt and pepper to taste, then spread into the prepared tin. Leave to set.

To make the tapenade, finely chop the sun-dried tomatoes, olives, capers and parsley. Mix with the garlic, lemon juice and oil, and season to taste.

Preheat the grill to high. Cut the polenta into 8 slices and arrange on a baking sheet with the cherry vine tomatoes. Brush with oil and grill until golden, turning once.

Serve the polenta slices topped with a spoonful of tapenade and the grilled tomatoes.

Energy (kcals): 280   Fat (of which saturated fat): 20 g (3 g)   Carbohydrate (of which sugar): 19 g (1.5 g)   Salt: 0.9 g

tabbouleh

serves 4

175 g/6 oz quinoa

600 ml/1 pint water

10 vine-ripened cherry
tomatoes, halved

7.5-cm/3-inch piece
cucumber, diced

3 spring onions,
sliced

juice of ½ lemon

2 tbsp extra virgin olive oil

4 tbsp chopped fresh mint

4 tbsp chopped fresh
coriander

4 tbsp chopped fresh
parsley

salt and pepper

Put the quinoa into a medium-sized saucepan and cover with
the water. Bring to the boil, then reduce the heat, cover and
simmer over a low heat for 15 minutes. Drain if necessary.

Leave the quinoa to cool slightly before combining with the
remaining ingredients in a salad bowl. Season to taste with salt
and pepper before serving.

Energy (kcals): 200   Fat (of which saturated fat): 8 g (1 g)   Carbohydrate (of which sugar): 25 g (5 g)   Salt: 0.1 g

pear salad

4 lean bacon rashers

75 g/2¾ oz walnut halves

2 Red William pears, cored
and sliced lengthways

1 tbsp lemon juice

175 g/6 oz watercress,
tough stalks removed

dressing

3 tbsp extra virgin olive oil

2 tbsp lemon juice

½ tsp clear honey

salt and pepper

Preheat the grill to high. Arrange the bacon on a foil-lined grill pan and cook under the preheated grill until well-browned and crisp. Set aside to cool, then cut into 1-cm/½-inch pieces.

Meanwhile, heat a dry frying pan over a medium heat and lightly toast the walnuts, shaking the pan frequently, for 3 minutes, or until lightly browned. Set aside to cool.

Toss the pears in the lemon juice to prevent discoloration. Put the watercress, walnuts, pears and bacon into a salad bowl.

To make the dressing, whisk the oil, lemon juice and honey together in a small bowl or jug. Season to taste with salt and pepper, then pour over the salad. Toss well to combine and serve.

Energy (kcals): 280   Fat (of which saturated fat): 23 g (3 g)   Carbohydrate (of which sugar): 9 g (9 g)   Salt: 0.9 g

spicy carrot soup

serves 4

2 tbsp olive oil

1 large onion, chopped

1 celery stick, chopped

1 potato, diced

6 carrots, sliced

1 tsp paprika

2 tsp ground cumin

1 tsp ground coriander

½ tsp chilli powder (optional)

175 g/6 oz red split lentils

1.2 litres/2 pints gluten-free vegetable or chicken stock

2 bay leaves

salt and pepper

2 tbsp chopped fresh coriander, to garnish

Heat the oil in a large, heavy-based saucepan over a medium–low heat. Add the onion and fry for 7 minutes, stirring occasionally. Add the celery, potato and carrots and cook for a further 5 minutes, stirring occasionally. Stir in the paprika, cumin, ground coriander and chilli powder, if using, and cook for a further minute.

Stir in the lentils, stock and bay leaves. Bring to the boil, then reduce the heat and simmer, half-covered, over a low heat, stirring occasionally to prevent the lentils sticking to the bottom of the saucepan, for 25 minutes, or until the lentils are tender.

Remove and discard the bay leaves. Transfer to a food processor or blender, or use a hand blender, and process the soup until thick and smooth. Return to the saucepan and reheat. Season to taste with salt and pepper and add extra chilli powder, if liked. Ladle into 4 warmed bowls and sprinkle with fresh coriander before serving.

Energy (kcals): 290   Fat (of which saturated fat): 7 g (1 g)   Carbohydrate (of which sugar): 46 g (14 g)   Salt: 0.15 g

tofu salad

serves 4

200 g/7 oz buckwheat noodles

250 g/9 oz firm smoked tofu

200 g/7 oz white cabbage, finely shredded

250 g/9 oz carrots, finely shredded

3 spring onions, diagonally sliced

1 fresh red chilli, deseeded and finely sliced

2 tbsp sesame seeds, lightly toasted, to garnish

dressing

1 tsp grated fresh ginger

1 garlic clove, crushed

175 g/6 oz silken tofu

4 tsp gluten-free tamari

2 tbsp sesame oil

4 tbsp hot water

salt

Cook the noodles in a large saucepan of lightly salted boiling water according to the packet instructions. Drain and refresh under cold running water.

To make the dressing, blend the ginger, garlic, silken tofu, tamari sauce, oil and water together in a small bowl until smooth and creamy. Season to taste with salt.

Place the smoked tofu in a steamer. Steam for 5 minutes, then cut into thin slices.

Meanwhile, put the cabbage, carrots, spring onions and chilli into a bowl and toss to mix. To serve, arrange the noodles on serving plates and top with the carrot salad and slices of tofu. Spoon over the dressing and garnish with sesame seeds.

Energy (kcals): 435   Fat (of which saturated fat): 20 g (4 g)   Carbohydrate (of which sugar): 43 g (9 g)   Salt: 1 g

chicken tacos

serves 4

1 ripe avocado

150 ml/5 fl oz plain
soya yogurt

2 tbsp medium cornmeal

1 tsp chilli powder

½ tsp dried thyme

600 g/1 lb 5 oz chicken
breasts, cut into
thin strips

2 tbsp sunflower oil

1 red onion, sliced

1 large red pepper,
deseeded and sliced

1 large green pepper,
deseeded and sliced

8 wheat- and gluten-free
taco shells

salt and pepper

smoked paprika, to garnish

Halve the avocado, remove the stone and scoop out the flesh, then purée in a blender with the yogurt. Season to taste with salt and pepper.

Mix together the cornmeal, chilli and thyme with salt and pepper in a large bowl. Add the chicken and toss to coat evenly.

Heat the oil in a wok or large frying pan and stir-fry the onion and peppers for 3–4 minutes to soften. Remove and keep hot.

Add the chicken and stir-fry for 5–6 minutes, until evenly browned. Return the vegetables to the pan and stir-fry for a further 1–2 minutes.

Spoon the chicken mixture into the taco shells and top with a spoonful of the avocado mixture. Sprinkle with smoked paprika and serve.

Energy (kcals): 465   Fat (of which saturated fat): 21 g (3 g)   Carbohydrate (of which sugar): 25 g (8 g)   Salt: 0.3 g

spring rolls

makes 16 rolls

2 tbsp gluten-free tamari

1½ tsp maple syrup

500 g/1 lb 2 oz lean
pork fillets

vegetable oil, for frying

32 rice paper pancakes

gluten-free hoisin sauce

70 g/2½ oz rice vermicelli
noodles, cooked

strips of cucumber

strips of spring onion

Blend the tamari and maple syrup together in a shallow dish. Add the pork and turn to coat in the mixture. Cover and leave to marinate in the refrigerator for at least 1 hour or preferably overnight.

Heat a griddle pan over a medium–high heat until hot, add a little oil to cover the base and cook the pork for 4–6 minutes each side, depending on the thickness of the fillets, until cooked and caramelized on the outside. Remove from the pan and slice into fine strips.

Fill a heatproof bowl with water that is just off the boil. Put 2 rice paper pancakes on top of one another (you will need 2 per roll as they are very thin and fragile) and soak in the water for 20 seconds, or until they turn pliable and opaque. Carefully remove using a spatula, drain for a second and place flat on a plate.

Spread a spoonful of hoisin sauce over the pancake and top with a small bundle of noodles and a few strips of pork, cucumber and spring onion. Fold in the ends and sides of the pancake to resemble a spring roll. Set aside while you make the remaining rolls. Slice in half on the diagonal and serve with a little more hoisin sauce, if liked.

Energy (kcals): 96   Fat (of which saturated fat): 3 g (0.5 g)   Carbohydrate (of which sugar): 8 g (1 g)   Salt: 0.4 g

sushi rolls

serves 4

4 sheets nori (seaweed)

wasabi (Japanese horseradish sauce)

gluten-free tamari

pink pickled ginger

rice

250 g/9 oz sushi rice

2 tbsp rice vinegar

1 tsp caster sugar

½ tsp salt

fillings

50 g/1¾ oz smoked salmon

4-cm/1½-inch piece cucumber, peeled, deseeded and cut into matchsticks

40 g/1½ oz cooked peeled prawns

1 small avocado, stoned, peeled, thinly sliced and tossed in lemon juice

Put the rice into a saucepan and cover with cold water. Bring to the boil, then reduce the heat, cover and simmer for 15–20 minutes, or until the rice is tender and the water has been absorbed. Drain if necessary and transfer to a bowl. Mix the vinegar, sugar and salt together, then, using a spatula, stir well into the rice. Cover with a damp cloth and leave to cool.

To make the rolls, lay a clean bamboo mat over a chopping board. Lay a sheet of nori, shiny side-down, on the mat. Spread a quarter of the rice mixture over the nori, using wet fingers to press it down evenly, leaving a 1-cm/½-inch margin at the top and bottom.

For smoked salmon and cucumber rolls, lay the salmon over the rice and arrange the cucumber in a line across the centre. For the prawn rolls, lay the prawns and avocado in a line across the centre.

Carefully hold the nearest edge of the mat, then, using the mat as a guide, roll up the nori tightly to make a neat tube of rice enclosing the filling. Seal the uncovered edge with a little water, then roll the sushi off the mat. Repeat to make 3 more rolls – you need 2 salmon and cucumber and 2 prawn and avocado in total. Using a wet knife, cut each roll into 8 pieces and stand upright on a platter. Wipe and rinse the knife between cuts to prevent the rice from sticking. Serve the rolls with wasabi, tamari and pickled ginger.

Energy (kcals): 312   Fat (of which saturated fat): 6.5 g (1 g)   Carbohydrate (of which sugar): 48 g (1.5 g)   Salt: 1.1 g

seafood pizza

serves 4

2 tbsp olive oil, plus extra for greasing

200 g/7 oz buckwheat flour

100 g/3½ oz rice flour

100 g/3½ oz potato flour

2 tsp xanthan gum

7 g/⅓ oz sachet gluten-free fast-action yeast

1 tsp salt

350 ml/12 fl oz tepid water

200 g/7 oz passata

2 shallots, finely chopped

2 tbsp chopped fresh dill

175 g/6 oz canned tuna in sunflower oil, drained and flaked

175 g/6 oz king prawns, cooked and peeled

280 g/10 oz artichokes in oil, drained

2 tbsp salted capers, rinsed

8 pitted black or green olives

salt and pepper

Brush a large baking sheet with oil. Mix the flours, xanthan gum, yeast and salt in a bowl, make a well in the centre and stir in the water with 1 tablespoon of oil to make a soft dough.

Knead the dough gently on a lightly floured surface for 4–5 minutes until smooth, then roll to a 33-cm/13-inch round on the prepared baking sheet, pushing the edges up slightly to make a raised edge. Cover and leave in a warm place for about 1½ hours, or until risen and doubled in size.

Preheat the oven to 200°C/400°F/Gas Mark 6. Spread the passata over the dough to within 1 cm/½ inch of the edge. Sprinkle over the shallots and 1 tablespoon of dill. Top with tuna, prawns, artichokes, capers and olives. Season and sprinkle with the remaining oil.

Bake in the preheated oven for 25–30 minutes. Sprinkle with the remaining dill and serve hot.

Energy (kcals): 621   Fat (of which saturated fat): 19 g (2.5 g)   Carbohydrate (of which sugar): 81 g (2.5 g)   Salt: 3.7 g

baba ghanoush

serves 6

1 large aubergine, pricked

3 fat garlic cloves, unpeeled

1 tsp ground coriander

1 tsp ground cumin

1 tbsp light tahini

juice of ½ lemon

2 tbsp extra virgin olive oil

salt and pepper

coriander, to garnish

flat breads

250 g/9 oz gluten-free
strong white flour

2 tbsp fine cornmeal

1 tsp gluten-free baking
powder

1 tsp salt

50 g/1¾ oz dairy-free
spread, diced

1 tbsp sesame seeds

150–175 ml/5–6 fl oz
warm water

sunflower oil, for oiling

To make the baba ghanoush, preheat the oven to 200°C/ 400°F/Gas Mark 6. Put the aubergine into a roasting tin and bake in the preheated oven for 25 minutes. Add the garlic cloves to the tin and cook for a further 15 minutes until the aubergine and garlic are very tender.

Halve the aubergine and scoop out the flesh with a spoon into a food processor or blender. Peel the garlic cloves and add to the food processor or blender with the spices, tahini, lemon juice and oil. Process until smooth and creamy, then season to taste with salt and pepper. Transfer to a serving dish and cover until required. Meanwhile, make the flat breads. Sift the flour, cornmeal, baking powder and salt into a mixing bowl, then rub in the spread until the mixture resembles breadcrumbs. Add the sesame seeds and stir in the water with your hands to bring the mixture together into a ball, adding more water or flour as necessary.

Turn the mixture out on to a lightly floured work surface and knead lightly until a soft dough forms. Divide into 6 pieces, then roll each piece into a ball. Wrap in clingfilm and leave to rest in the refrigerator for 30 minutes. Roll out or press the dough balls with your fingers into 5-mm/¼-inch thick rounds. Heat a lightly oiled griddle pan over a medium heat and cook each flat bread for a few minutes on each side until lightly golden. Garnish the baba ghanoush with coriander and serve with the warm flat breads.

Energy (kcals): 308   Fat (of which saturated fat): 16 g (3 g)   Carbohydrate (of which sugar): 36 g (1 g)   Salt: 1.3 g

vegetable tempura

serves 4

ginger tofu dip

250 g/9 oz soft silken tofu, drained

2-cm/¾-inch piece ginger, chopped

1 small shallot, chopped

1 garlic clove, crushed

1 tbsp gluten-free tamari

2 tsp rice vinegar

batter

150 g/5½ oz gluten-free plain white flour blend

1 egg

200 ml/7 fl oz iced water

sunflower oil, for deep-frying

500 g/1 lb 2 oz vegetables, e.g. asparagus tips, baby carrots, mangetout, baby corn, mushrooms, broccoli florets

salt and pepper

For the dip, place all the ingredients in a food processor, or use a hand blender, and process until smooth.

For the batter, beat together the flour, egg, water and salt and pepper to make a smooth, bubbly batter.

Heat a deep pan of oil to 180°C/350°F, or until a small cube of bread browns in 30 seconds. Dip the vegetables quickly into the batter, then deep-fry in batches for 1–2 minutes until they are crisp and rise to the surface. Drain on kitchen paper and keep hot.

Serve the vegetables immediately, with the dip.

Energy (kcals): 353   Fat (of which saturated fat): 17.5 g (2.5 g)   Carbohydrate (of which sugar): 34 g (4.5 g)   Salt: 1 g

spicy falafels

serves 4

400 g/14 oz canned chickpeas, drained

1 small red onion, chopped

2 garlic cloves, crushed

2 tsp ground coriander

1½ tsp ground cumin

1 tsp ground star anise

1 red chilli, chopped

1 egg white

½ tsp gluten-free baking powder

gram flour, for shaping

sunflower oil, for deep-frying

salt and pepper

salad

1 large orange

2 tbsp extra virgin olive oil

55 g/2 oz rocket leaves

Place the chickpeas, onion, garlic, coriander, cumin, anise, chilli, egg white and salt and pepper in a food processor and process to a fairly firm paste, but still with some texture. Stir in the baking powder.

Use a little gram flour on your hands to shape the mixture into about 12 small balls.

To make the salad, cut all the peel and white pith from the orange and lift out the segments, catching the juice. Whisk the juice with the olive oil and season to taste. Lightly toss the orange segments and rocket with the dressing.

Heat a 2.5-cm/1-inch depth of oil in a large pan to 180°C/350°F, or until a cube of bread browns in 30 seconds. Fry the falafels for about 2 minutes, turning until golden brown.

Drain the falafels on kitchen paper and serve with the salad.

Energy (kcals): 300   Fat (of which saturated fat): 24 g (3 g)   Carbohydrate (of which sugar): 15 g (5.5 g)   Salt: 0.5 g

basil gnocchi

serves 4

500 g/1 lb 2 oz floury potatoes (e.g. Maris Piper)

3 tbsp finely chopped basil

½ tsp ground nutmeg

100 g/3½ oz gluten-free and wheat-free plain white flour blend, plus extra for dusting

1 small egg, beaten

4 plum tomatoes, halved

1 medium red onion, halved

2 garlic cloves

oil, for brushing

salt and pepper

basil leaves, to garnish

Peel the potatoes and cut into chunks. Cook in lightly salted, boiling water for 15–20 minutes or until tender. Drain thoroughly.

Press the potatoes through a potato ricer or coarse sieve. Add the chopped basil and season well with nutmeg and salt and pepper. Lightly stir in the flour and add enough egg to make a fairly soft, but not sticky, dough.

Divide the dough into four and roll each piece to a sausage about 20-cm/8-inch long, 2.5-cm/1-inch wide. Cut each into 8–9 slices. Roll each into a ball and press over a floured fork with your thumb, making ridges on one side and an indentation on the other.

Preheat a grill to hot. Place the tomatoes and onion cut side down onto a baking sheet with the garlic cloves and brush with oil. Grill for 8–10 minutes until the skins are charred. Remove the skins and roughly chop.

Bring a large pan of water to the boil, and cook the gnocchi in batches for 4–6 minutes, or until they rise to the surface. Lift out with a slotted spoon.

Serve the gnocchi hot, with the tomato sauce spooned over and garnish with basil leaves.

Energy (kcals): 240   Fat (of which saturated fat): 4 g (0.8 g)   Carbohydrate (of which sugar): 45 g (5 g)   Salt: 0.3 g

courgette quiche

serves 4

pastry

200 g/7 oz gluten- and wheat-free plain white flour blend

100 g/3½ oz dairy-free soya spread

3 tbsp chopped chives

4–5 tbsp cold water

salt

filling

2 tbsp olive oil

1 small red onion, cut into wedges

2 medium courgettes, cut into 2-cm/¾-inch chunks

8 cherry tomatoes, halved

1 large egg, beaten

175 ml/6 fl oz unsweetened dairy-free soya milk

salt and pepper

For the pastry, place the flour, spread and chives with a pinch of salt in a food processor and process to fine crumbs. Mix in just enough water to bind the mixture to a firm dough.

Roll out on a lightly floured surface to line a 19-cm/7½-inch diameter, 5-cm/2¾-inch deep, loose-based flan tin. Prick the base with a fork and chill in the refrigerator for 10 minutes.

Preheat the oven to 200°C/400°C/Gas Mark 6 and preheat a baking sheet. Line the pastry case with baking paper and dried beans and bake blind in the preheated oven for 10 minutes. Remove the paper and beans and bake for a further 5 minutes. Reduce the oven temperature to 190°C/375°F/Gas Mark 5.

For the filling, heat the oil and fry the onion and courgettes, stirring often, for 4–5 minutes, or until softened and lightly browned. Tip into the pastry case with the tomatoes.

Beat the egg with the milk and season well. Pour into the pastry case. Bake in the preheated oven for 35–40 minutes, or until golden brown and set. Cool for 10 minutes before turning out. Serve the quiche warm or cold.

Energy (kcals): 464   Fat (of which saturated fat): 30 g (6 g)   Carbohydrate (of which sugar): 41 g (3 g)   Salt: 0.9 g

3

Main Meals

mushroom pasta

serves 4

300 g/10½ oz dried gluten-free penne or pasta shape of your choice

2 tbsp olive oil

250 g/9 oz mushrooms, sliced

1 tsp dried oregano

250 ml/9 fl oz gluten-free vegetable stock

1 tbsp lemon juice

6 tbsp vegan cream cheese

200 g/7 oz frozen spinach leaves

salt and pepper

Cook the pasta in a large saucepan of lightly salted boiling water according to the packet instructions. Drain, reserving 175 ml/6 fl oz of the cooking liquid.

Meanwhile, heat the oil in a large, heavy-based frying pan over a medium heat, add the mushrooms and cook, stirring frequently, for 8 minutes, or until almost crisp. Stir in the oregano, stock and lemon juice and cook for 10–12 minutes, or until the sauce is reduced by half.

Stir in the cream cheese and spinach and cook over a medium–low heat for 3–5 minutes. Add the reserved cooking liquid, then the cooked pasta. Stir well, season to taste with salt and pepper and heat through before serving.

Energy (kcals): 400   Fat (of which saturated fat): 14 g (3 g)   Carbohydrate (of which sugar): 59 g (4 g)   Salt: 0.4 g

haddock flan

serves 6

400 g/14 oz undyed smoked haddock or cod fillet, rinsed and dried

300 ml/10 fl oz dairy-free milk

150 g/5½ oz cooked peeled prawns

200 g/7 oz vegan cream cheese

3 eggs, beaten

3 tbsp snipped fresh chives

pepper

pastry

200 g/7 oz gluten-free plain flour

large pinch of salt

100 g/3½ oz dairy-free spread, diced, plus extra for greasing

1 egg yolk

3 tbsp ice-cold water

Preheat the oven to 200°C/400°F/Gas Mark 6. Lightly grease a 26-cm/10½-inch flan dish.

To make the pastry, sift the flour and salt into a mixing bowl, then rub in the spread with your fingertips until the mixture resembles coarse breadcrumbs. Stir in the egg yolk, followed by the water, then bring the dough together into a ball. Turn out onto a lightly floured work surface and knead until smooth. Wrap in clingfilm and chill in the refrigerator for 30 minutes.

Meanwhile, put the fish into a shallow saucepan with the milk. Heat gently until simmering and simmer for 10 minutes, or until just cooked and opaque. Remove the fish with a slotted spoon, leave to cool a little, then peel away the skin and discard any bones. Flake the fish into large chunks and set aside. Reserve 125 ml/4 fl oz of the cooking liquid.

Roll out the pastry and use to line the prepared flan dish. Line the pastry case with baking paper and dried beans and bake in the preheated oven for 8 minutes. Remove the paper and beans and bake for a further 5 minutes.

Arrange the fish and prawns in the pastry case. Beat together the cream cheese, reserved cooking liquid, eggs, chives and pepper to taste in a bowl, then pour over the seafood. Bake for 30 minutes, or until the filling is set and golden brown.

Energy (kcals): 533   Fat (of which saturated fat): 36 g (14 g)   Carbohydrate (of which sugar): 25 g (0.5 g)   Salt: 2.6 g

baked lemon cod

serves 4

4 thick cod fillets

olive oil, for brushing

8 thin lemon slices

salt and pepper

herb sauce

4 tbsp olive oil

1 garlic clove, crushed

4 tbsp chopped fresh parsley

2 tbsp chopped fresh mint

juice of ½ lemon

salt and pepper

Preheat the oven to 200°C/400°F/Gas Mark 6. Rinse each cod fillet and pat dry with kitchen paper, then brush with oil. Place each fillet on a piece of baking paper that is large enough to encase the fish in a parcel. Top each fillet with 2 lemon slices and season to taste with salt and pepper. Fold over the baking paper to encase the fish and bake in the preheated oven for 20 minutes, or until just cooked and opaque.

Meanwhile, to make the herb sauce, put all the ingredients into a food processor and process until finely chopped. Season to taste with salt and pepper.

Carefully unfold each parcel and place on serving plates. Pour a spoonful of herb sauce over each piece of fish before serving.

Energy (kcals): 232   Fat (of which saturated fat): 13.5 g (2 g)   Carbohydrate (of which sugar): 0 g (0 g)   Salt: 0.23 g

prawn noodles

serves 4

2 tbsp vegetable oil

1 small red pepper, deseeded and diced

200 g/7 oz pak choi, stalks thinly sliced and leaves left whole

2 large garlic cloves, chopped

1 tsp ground turmeric

2 tsp garam masala

1 tsp chilli powder (optional)

125 ml/4 fl oz hot gluten-free vegetable stock

2 heaped tbsp smooth peanut butter

350 ml/12 fl oz coconut milk

1 tbsp gluten-free tamari

250 g/9 oz thick rice noodles

280 g/10 oz cooked peeled large prawns

Heat the oil in a wok or large, heavy-based frying pan over a high heat. Add the red pepper, pak choi stalks and garlic and stir-fry for 3 minutes. Add the turmeric, garam masala, chilli powder, if using, and pak choi leaves and stir-fry for a further minute.

Mix the hot stock and peanut butter together in a heatproof bowl until the peanut butter has dissolved, then add to the stir-fry with the coconut milk and tamari. Cook for 5 minutes over a medium heat, or until reduced and thickened.

Meanwhile, immerse the noodles in a bowl of just boiled water. Leave for 4 minutes, then drain and refresh the noodles under cold running water. Add the cooked noodles and prawns to the coconut curry and cook for a further 2–3 minutes, stirring frequently, until heated through.

Transfer to bowls and serve.

Energy (kcals): 564   Fat (of which saturated fat): 26 g (15 g)   Carbohydrate (of which sugar): 55 g (3 g)   Salt: 1.9 g

salmon fingers

serves 3

150 g/5 oz fine cornmeal or polenta

1 tsp paprika

400 g/14 oz salmon fillet, skinned and sliced into 12 chunky fingers

1 egg, beaten

sunflower oil, for frying

potato wedges

500 g/1 lb 2 oz potatoes, scrubbed and cut into thick wedges

1–2 tbsp olive oil

½ tsp paprika

salt

Preheat the oven to 200°C/400°F/Gas Mark 6. To make the wedges, dry the potato wedges on a clean tea towel. Spoon the oil into a roasting tin and put into the preheated oven briefly to heat. Toss the potatoes in the warm oil until well coated. Sprinkle with paprika and salt to taste and roast for 30 minutes, turning halfway through, until crisp and golden.

Meanwhile, mix the cornmeal and paprika together on a plate. Dip each salmon finger into the beaten egg, then roll in the cornmeal mixture until evenly coated.

Heat enough oil to cover the base of a large, heavy-based frying pan over a medium heat. Carefully arrange half the salmon fingers in the pan and cook for 6 minutes, turning halfway through, until golden. Drain on kitchen paper and keep warm while you cook the remaining fingers. Serve with the potato wedges.

Energy (kcals): 677   Fat (of which saturated fat): 30 g (4.5 g)   Carbohydrate (of which sugar): 61 g (1 g)   Salt: 0.25 g

beef stew

serves 4

3 tbsp gluten-free
plain flour

800 g/1 lb 12 oz braising
steak, cubed

3 tbsp olive oil

12 shallots, halved

2 carrots, cut into batons

1 parsnip, sliced

2 bay leaves

1 tbsp fresh rosemary

450 ml/16 fl oz cider

250 ml/9 fl oz gluten-free
beef stock

1 tbsp gluten-free tamari

200 g/7 oz canned
chestnuts, drained

115 g/4 oz gluten-free self-
raising flour, plus extra
for flouring

50 g/1¾ oz gluten-free
vegetable suet

2 tbsp fresh thyme

salt and pepper

Preheat the oven to 160°C/325°F/Gas Mark 3. Put the flour into a clean polythene bag or on a plate and season generously with salt and pepper. Toss the beef in the seasoned flour until coated. Heat 1 tablespoon of the oil in a large, flameproof casserole dish over a medium–high heat. Add one-third of the beef and cook for 5–6 minutes, turning occasionally, until browned all over – the meat may stick to the casserole dish until it is properly sealed. Remove the beef with a slotted spoon. Cook the remaining 2 batches, adding another tablespoon of oil as necessary. Set aside when all the beef has been sealed. Add the remaining oil to the casserole dish with the shallots, carrots, parsnip, bay leaves and rosemary and cook for 3 minutes, stirring occasionally. Pour in the cider and beef stock and bring to the boil. Cook over a high heat until the alcohol has evaporated and the liquid reduced. Add the tamari, then cook for a further 3 minutes. Stir in the chestnuts and beef, cover and cook in the preheated oven for 1 hour 35 minutes.

Meanwhile, to make the dumplings, combine the flour, suet and thyme in a bowl and season to taste with salt and pepper. Mix in enough water to make a soft dough. Divide the dough into walnut-sized pieces and, using floured hands, roll each piece into a ball. Add to the casserole dish, cover and cook for a further 25 minutes, or until the dumplings are cooked, the stock has formed a thick, rich gravy and the meat is tender. Season to taste with salt and pepper before serving.

Energy (kcals): 709   Fat (of which saturated fat): 32 g (12 g)   Carbohydrate (of which sugar): 47 g (13.5 g)   Salt: 2 g

meatball pasta

serves 4

300 g/10½ oz dried
gluten-free spaghetti

salt and pepper

meatballs

40 g/1½ oz fresh gluten-
free breadcrumbs

450 g/1 lb fresh lean beef
mince

1 onion, grated

1 large garlic clove, crushed

1 egg, beaten

salt and pepper

tomato sauce

1 tbsp olive oil

2 garlic cloves, chopped

2 tsp dried oregano

300 ml/10 fl oz dry
white wine

600 ml/1 pint passata

1 bay leaf

2 tsp tomato purée

½ tsp sugar

To make the meatballs, put the breadcrumbs, mince, onion, garlic and egg into a bowl and mix well until combined. Season to taste with salt and pepper, cover and chill in the refrigerator for 30 minutes.

Meanwhile, make the tomato sauce. Heat the oil in a large, heavy-based frying pan over a medium heat and fry the garlic, stirring, for 1 minute. Add the oregano and cook, stirring, for a further minute. Pour in the wine and cook over a high heat until it has almost evaporated.

Add the passata, bay leaf, tomato purée and sugar, then stir well. Partially cover the pan and cook over a medium–low heat for 5 minutes.

Form the meatball mixture into walnut-sized balls. Add to the sauce, partially cover and cook for 15–20 minutes, or until the meatballs are cooked through.

Meanwhile, cook the spaghetti in a large saucepan of lightly salted boiling water according to the packet instructions. Drain, reserving 3 tablespoons of the cooking liquid. Stir the cooking liquid into the sauce before serving with the pasta.

Energy (kcals): 640   Fat (of which saturated fat): 17 g (5.9 g)   Carbohydrate (of which sugar): 70 g (5 g)   Salt: 0.5 g

lamb koftas

serves 4

250 g/9 oz fresh lean lamb mince

1 onion, finely chopped

1 tbsp chopped fresh coriander

1 tbsp chopped fresh parsley

½ tsp ground coriander

¼ tsp chilli powder

oil, for brushing

salt and pepper

chickpea mash

1 tbsp olive oil

2 garlic cloves, chopped

400 g/14 oz canned chickpeas, drained and rinsed

50 ml/2 fl oz dairy-free milk

2 tbsp chopped fresh coriander

salt and pepper

coriander sprigs, to garnish

Put the lamb, onion, herbs, spices and salt and pepper to taste in a food processor. Process until thoroughly combined.

Divide the mixture into 12 portions and, using wet hands, shape each portion into a sausage shape around a wooden skewer (soaked in water first to prevent burning). Cover and chill the skewers in the refrigerator for 30 minutes.

To cook, preheat a griddle pan over a medium heat and brush with a little oil. Cook the skewers in 2 batches, turning occasionally, for 10 minutes, or until browned on all sides and cooked through.

To make the chickpea mash, heat the oil in a saucepan and gently fry the garlic for 2 minutes. Add the chickpeas and milk and heat through for a few minutes. Transfer to a food processor or blender and process until smooth. Season to taste with salt and pepper, then stir in the fresh coriander. Garnish with coriander sprigs and serve with the koftas.

Energy (kcals): 222   Fat (of which saturated fat): 12 g (4 g)   Carbohydrate (of which sugar): 11 g (1.5 g)   Salt: 0.5 g

pork pies

serves 4

2 tbsp sunflower oil

6 shallots, cut into wedges

600 g/1 lb 5 oz diced
lean pork

250 g/9 oz chestnut
mushrooms, quartered

150 ml/5 fl oz apple juice

1 tbsp chopped tarragon

salt and pepper

pastry

400 g/14 oz potatoes,
cut into even chunks

85 g/3 oz dairy-free olive
spread

2 tsp chopped tarragon

125 g/4½ oz rice flour

1 tsp gluten-free baking
powder

beaten egg, to glaze

salt and pepper

Preheat the oven to 200°C/400°F/Gas Mark 6. Heat the oil in a large pan and fry the shallots for 2–3 minutes, stirring occasionally.

Add the pork and fry for 6–8 minutes, stirring, until browned. Add the mushrooms and cook for 2 minutes to soften.

Stir in the apple juice, tarragon and seasoning. Divide the mixture between four 300-ml/10-fl oz ovenproof dishes.

To make the pastry, cook the potatoes in lightly salted, boiling water until tender. Drain thoroughly and cool, uncovered.

Mash the potatoes, then stir in the spread, tarragon and salt and pepper. Sift over the rice flour and baking powder and stir in lightly and evenly to make a soft dough, pressing together with your hands.

Divide the dough into four and roll out each to cover the pie dishes, pinching the edges to seal.

Place the pies on a baking sheet, brush the tops with egg and bake for 35–40 minutes, until golden. Serve hot.

Energy (kcals): 624   Fat (of which saturated fat): 31 g (7 g)   Carbohydrate (of which sugar): 48 g (5.5 g)   Salt: 0.9 g

chicken curry

serves 4

2 tbsp vegetable oil

4 skinless chicken breasts, 800 g/1 lb 12 oz in total, cut into 2.5-cm/1-inch pieces

1½ tsp cumin seeds

1 large onion, grated

2 fresh green chillies, finely chopped

2 large garlic cloves, grated

1 tbsp grated fresh ginger

1 tsp ground turmeric

1 tsp ground coriander

1 tsp garam masala

300 ml/10 fl oz coconut milk

250 ml/9 fl oz canned chopped tomatoes

2 tsp lemon juice

salt

2 tbsp chopped fresh coriander, to garnish

cooked basmati rice, to serve

Heat the oil in a large, heavy-based saucepan over a medium heat. Add the chicken and cook for 5–8 minutes, turning frequently, until lightly browned and cooked through. Remove from the saucepan and set aside. Add the cumin seeds and cook until they begin to darken and sizzle. Stir in the onion, partially cover and cook over a medium–low heat, stirring frequently, for 10 minutes, or until soft and golden. Add the chillies, garlic, ginger, turmeric, ground coriander and garam masala and cook for 1 minute.

Return the chicken to the saucepan and stir in the coconut milk and tomatoes. Partially cover and cook over a medium heat for 15 minutes until the sauce has reduced and thickened. Stir in the lemon juice and season to taste with salt.

Serve the curry with the basmati rice, sprinkled with fresh coriander.

Energy (kcals): 424   Fat (of which saturated fat): 21 g (12.5 g)   Carbohydrate (of which sugar): 8.5 g (4 g)   Salt: 0.4 g

roast chicken

serves 4

4 skinless, boneless chicken breasts, about 800 g/1 lb 12 oz in total

1 tbsp olive oil

pesto

125 g/4½ oz sun-blush tomatoes in oil (drained weight), chopped

2 garlic cloves, crushed

6 tbsp pine kernels, lightly toasted

150 ml/5 fl oz extra virgin olive oil

Preheat the oven to 200°C/400°F/Gas Mark 6. To make the red pesto, put the sun-blush tomatoes, garlic, 4 tablespoons of the pine kernels and oil into a food processor and process to a coarse paste.

Arrange the chicken in a large, ovenproof dish or roasting tin. Brush each breast with the oil, then place a tablespoon of pesto over each breast. Using the back of a spoon, spread the pesto so that it covers the top of each breast. This pesto recipe makes more than just the 4 tablespoons used here. Store the extra pesto in an airtight container in the refrigerator for up to 1 week.

Roast the chicken in the preheated oven for 30 minutes, or until tender and the juices run clear when a skewer is inserted into the thickest part of the meat.

Serve sprinkled with the remaining toasted pine kernels.

Energy (kcals): 690   Fat (of which saturated fat): 51 g (6 g)   Carbohydrate (of which sugar): 5 g (4 g)   Salt: 0.8 g

squash risotto

serves 4

600 g/1 lb 5 oz butternut
squash or pumpkin,
peeled and cut into
bite-sized pieces

4 tbsp olive oil

1 tsp clear honey

25 g/1 oz fresh basil

25 g/1 oz fresh oregano

1 tbsp dairy-free spread

2 onions, finely chopped

450 g/1 lb arborio or other
risotto rice

175 ml/6 fl oz dry
white wine

1.2 litres/2 pints gluten-
free vegetable stock

salt and pepper

Preheat the oven to 200°C/400°F/Gas Mark 6. Put the squash into a roasting tin. Mix 1 tablespoon of the oil with the honey and spoon over the squash. Turn the squash to coat it in the mixture. Roast in the preheated oven for 30–35 minutes, or until tender.

Meanwhile, put the basil and oregano into a food processor with 2 tablespoons of the remaining oil and process until finely chopped and blended. Set aside.

Heat the spread and remaining oil in a large, heavy-based saucepan over a medium heat. Add the onions and fry, stirring occasionally, for 8 minutes, or until soft and golden. Add the rice and cook for 2 minutes, stirring to coat the grains in the oil mixture.

Pour in the wine and bring to the boil. Reduce the heat slightly and cook until the wine is almost absorbed. Add the stock, a little at a time, and cook over a medium–low heat, stirring constantly, for 20 minutes.

Gently stir in the herb oil and squash until thoroughly mixed into the rice and cook for a further 5 minutes, or until the rice is creamy and cooked but retaining a little bite in the centre of the grain. Season well with salt and pepper before serving.

Energy (kcals): 652   Fat (of which saturated fat): 15.5 g (2.5 g)   Carbohydrate (of which sugar): 108 g (11 g)   Salt: 0.5 g

thai tofu cakes

makes 8

300 g/10½ oz firm tofu (drained weight), coarsely grated

1 lemon grass stalk, outer layer discarded, finely chopped

2 garlic cloves, chopped

2.5-cm/1-inch piece fresh ginger, grated

2 kaffir lime leaves, finely chopped (optional)

2 shallots, finely chopped

2 fresh red chillies, deseeded and finely chopped

4 tbsp chopped fresh coriander

90 g/3¼ oz gluten-free plain flour, plus extra for flouring

½ tsp salt

sunflower oil, for frying

gluten-free sweet chilli dipping sauce, to serve

Mix the tofu with the lemon grass, garlic, ginger, lime leaves, if using, shallots, chillies and coriander in a mixing bowl. Stir in the flour and salt to make a coarse, sticky paste. Cover and chill in the refrigerator for 1 hour to allow the mixture to firm up slightly.

Form the mixture into large walnut-sized balls and, using floured hands, flatten into rounds until you have 8 cakes. Heat enough oil to cover the base of a large, heavy-based frying pan over a medium heat. Cook the cakes in 2 batches, turning halfway through, for 4–6 minutes, or until golden brown. Drain on kitchen paper and serve warm with the chilli dip.

Energy (kcals): 103   Fat (of which saturated fat): 5 g (0.7 g)   Carbohydrate (of which sugar): 10 g (0.3 g)   Salt: 0.3 g

aubergine tagine

serves 4

1 aubergine, cubed

3 tbsp olive oil

1 large onion, thinly sliced

1 carrot, diced

2 garlic cloves, chopped

115 g/4 oz mushrooms, sliced

2 tsp ground coriander

2 tsp cumin seeds

1 tsp chilli powder

1 tsp ground turmeric

600 ml/1 pint canned chopped tomatoes

300 ml/10 fl oz gluten-free vegetable stock

70 g/2½ oz no soak dried apricots, chopped

400 g/14 oz canned chickpeas, drained

1.2 litres/2 pints hot gluten-free vegetable stock

200 g/7 oz instant polenta

2 tbsp coriander, to garnish

Preheat the grill to medium. Toss the aubergine in 1 tablespoon of the oil and arrange in the grill pan. Cook under the preheated grill for 20 minutes, turning occasionally, until softened and beginning to blacken around the edges – brush with more oil if the aubergine becomes too dry.

Heat the remaining oil in a large, heavy-based saucepan over a medium heat. Add the onion and fry, stirring occasionally, for 8 minutes, or until soft and golden. Add the carrot, garlic and mushrooms and cook for 5 minutes. Add the spices and cook, stirring constantly, for a further minute.

Add the tomatoes and stock, stir well and bring to the boil. Reduce the heat and simmer for 10 minutes, or until the sauce begins to thicken and reduce.

Add the aubergine, apricots and chickpeas, partially cover and cook for a further 10 minutes, stirring occasionally.

Meanwhile, to make the polenta, pour the hot stock into a non-stick saucepan and bring to the boil. Pour in the polenta in a steady stream, stirring constantly with a wooden spoon. Reduce the heat to low and cook for 1–2 minutes, or until the polenta thickens to a mashed potato-like consistency. Serve the tagine with the polenta, sprinkled with the fresh coriander.

Energy (kcals): 440   Fat (of which saturated fat): 12 g (1.5 g)   Carbohydrate (of which sugar): 65 g (16 g)   Salt: 0.2 g

spicy sea bass

serves 4

4 large or 8 small sea bass fillets, about 650 g/ 1 lb 7 oz total weight

1 egg white

2 tbsp sunflower oil, for frying

mixed salad leaves, to serve

spice-crust

1½ tbsp coriander seeds

1 tbsp cumin seeds

2 tsp fennel seeds

1 tsp black peppercorns

½ tsp salt

cucumber sauce

7.5-cm/3-inch piece cucumber

100 g/3½ oz plain soya yogurt

2 tbsp chopped fresh mint

salt and pepper

To make the spice-crust, crush the coriander, cumin, fennel, peppercorns and salt in a pestle and mortar or spice mill. Tip into a wide dish and mix evenly.

Brush the fish fillets with egg white then press into the spice mixture to coat evenly. If time allows, cover and leave to marinate in the refrigerator for about 30 minutes.

To make the cucumber sauce, coarsely grate the cucumber and sprinkle lightly with salt. Leave to stand for 10 minutes then rinse and dry. Stir into the yogurt and add the mint with seasoning to taste.

Heat the oil in a wide, heavy-based frying pan and fry the fish on a fairly high heat for 4–6 minutes depending on thickness, turning once, until golden and just cooked through.

Drain the fish on kitchen paper and serve immediately with the cucumber sauce and mixed salad leaves.

Energy (kcals): 229   Fat (of which saturated fat): 12 g (1.5 g)   Carbohydrate (of which sugar): 1 g (1 g)   Salt: 0.9 g

spanish tortilla

serves 4

350 g/12 oz potatoes, cut into bite-sized cubes

1 tbsp olive oil

15 g/½ oz dairy-free spread

1 onion, thinly sliced

6 eggs, lightly beaten

salt and pepper

Cook the potatoes in a saucepan of salted boiling water for 10–12 minutes, or until tender. Drain well and set aside.

Meanwhile, heat the oil and spread in a medium-sized frying pan with a heatproof handle over a medium heat. Add the onion and fry, stirring occasionally, for 8 minutes, or until soft and golden. Add the potatoes and cook for a further 5 minutes, stirring to prevent them sticking. Spread the onions and potatoes evenly over the base of the pan.

Preheat the grill to medium. Season the eggs to taste with salt and pepper and pour over the onion and potatoes. Cook over a medium heat for 5–6 minutes, or until the eggs are just set and the base of the tortilla is lightly golden.

Place the pan under the preheated grill (if the handle is not heatproof, wrap with a double layer of foil) and cook the top of the tortilla for 2–3 minutes until it is just set and risen. Cut into wedges to serve.

Energy (kcals): 258   Fat (of which saturated fat): 16 g (4 g)   Carbohydrate (of which sugar): 17 g (2 g)   Salt: 0.4 g

vegetable curry

serves 4

200 g/7 oz carrots

300 g/10½ oz potatoes

2 tbsp vegetable oil

1½ tsp cumin seeds

seeds from 5 green
cardamom pods

1½ tsp mustard seeds

2 onions, grated

1 tsp ground turmeric

1 tsp ground coriander

1 bay leaf

1½ tsp chilli powder

1 tbsp grated fresh ginger

2 garlic cloves, crushed

250 ml/9 fl oz passata

200 ml/7 fl oz gluten-free
vegetable stock

115 g/4 oz frozen peas

115 g/4 oz frozen
spinach leaves

salt

8 wheat- and gluten-free
pancakes

Put the carrots and potatoes into a steamer and steam until just tender but retaining some bite.

Heat the oil in a large, heavy-based saucepan over a medium heat and add the cumin seeds, cardamom seeds and mustard seeds. When they begin to darken and sizzle, add the onions, partially cover and cook over a medium–low heat, stirring frequently, for 10 minutes.

Add the other spices, ginger and garlic and cook, stirring constantly, for 1 minute. Add the passata, stock, potatoes and carrots, partially cover and cook for 10–15 minutes, or until the vegetables are tender. Add the peas and spinach, then cook for a further 2–3 minutes. Season to taste with salt before serving with the pancakes.

Energy (kcals): 418   Fat (of which saturated fat): 15 g (2 g)   Carbohydrate (of which sugar): 56 g (9 g)   Salt: 1.8 g

vegetable röstis

serves 4

900 g/2 lb potatoes

sunflower oil, for frying

salt

vegan pesto dressing

2 tbsp vegan pesto

1 tbsp boiling water

1 tbsp extra virgin olive oil

roasted vegetables

2 tbsp extra virgin olive oil

1 tbsp balsamic vinegar

1 tsp clear honey

1 red pepper, deseeded
and quartered

2 courgettes, sliced

2 red onions, quartered

1 small fennel bulb,
cut into thin wedges

16 vine-ripened tomatoes

8 garlic cloves

2 fresh rosemary sprigs

For the roasted vegetables, mix the oil, vinegar and honey together in a large, shallow dish. Add the red pepper, courgettes, onions, fennel, tomatoes, garlic and rosemary to the dish and toss in the marinade. Leave to marinate for at least 1 hour.

Preheat the oven to 200°C/400°F/Gas Mark 6. Cook the potatoes in a saucepan of lightly salted boiling water for 8–10 minutes, or until partially cooked. Leave to cool, then coarsely grate.

Transfer the vegetables, except the tomatoes and garlic, and the marinade to a roasting tin. Roast in the preheated oven for 25 minutes, then add the tomatoes and garlic and roast for a further 15 minutes, or until the vegetables are tender and slightly blackened around the edges.

Meanwhile, cook the rösti. Take a quarter of the grated potato in your hands and form into a roughly shaped cake. Heat just enough oil to cover the base of a frying pan over a medium heat. Put the cakes, 2 at a time, into the pan and flatten with a spatula to form rounds about 2 cm/¾ inch thick.

Cook the rösti for 6 minutes on each side, or until golden brown and crisp. Mix together the dressing ingredients. To serve, top each rösti with the roasted vegetables and drizzle with a little pesto dressing.

Energy (kcals): 391   Fat (of which saturated fat): 19 g (2 g)   Carbohydrate (of which sugar): 51 g (11 g)   Salt: 0.1 g

4

Desserts & Baking

coconut macaroons

makes about 26

55 g/2 oz skinned pistachio nuts

40 g/1½ oz icing sugar

1 tbsp rice flour

2 egg whites

55 g/2 oz caster sugar

55 g/2 oz desiccated coconut

1 tbsp chopped mint

pistachios, to decorate

Preheat the oven to 180°C/350°F/Gas Mark 4. Line 2 baking sheets with baking paper.

Place the pistachio nuts, icing sugar and rice flour in a food processor and process until finely ground.

Whisk the egg whites in a clean, dry bowl until stiff, then gradually whisk in the caster sugar. Fold in the pistachio mixture, coconut and mint.

Spoon the mixture in small rocky heaps onto the baking sheets and press a pistachio on top of each.

Bake for about 20 minutes, until firm and just beginning to brown. Cool on the baking sheet and serve.

Energy (kcals): 42   Fat (of which saturated fat): 2.5 g (1.5 g)   Carbohydrate (of which sugar): 4 g (4 g)   Salt: Trace

mocha brownies

makes 12 brownies

100 g/3½ oz dairy-free spread, plus extra for greasing

150 g/5½ oz good-quality plain dark chocolate (about 70 per cent cocoa solids)

1 tsp strong instant coffee

1 tsp vanilla extract

100 g/3½ oz ground almonds

175 g/6 oz caster sugar

4 eggs, separated

icing sugar, to decorate (optional)

Preheat the oven to 180°C/350°F/Gas Mark 4. Grease a 20-cm/8-inch square cake tin and line the base.

Melt the chocolate and spread in a heatproof bowl placed over a saucepan of gently simmering water, making sure that the bottom of the bowl does not touch the water. Stir very occasionally until the chocolate and spread have melted and are smooth.

Carefully remove the bowl from the heat. Leave to cool slightly, then stir in the coffee and vanilla extract. Add the almonds and sugar and mix well until combined. Lightly beat the egg yolks in a separate bowl, then stir into the chocolate mixture.

Whisk the egg whites in a large bowl until they form stiff peaks. Gently fold a large spoonful of the egg whites into the chocolate mixture, then fold in the remainder until completely incorporated.

Spoon the mixture into the prepared tin and bake in the preheated oven for 35–40 minutes, or until risen and firm on top but still slightly gooey in the centre. Leave to cool in the tin, then turn out, remove the lining paper and cut into 12 pieces. Dust with icing sugar before serving, if liked.

Energy (kcals): 270   Fat (of which saturated fat): 18 g (4.5 g)   Carbohydrate (of which sugar): 22 g (22 g)   Salt: 0.3 g

orange cake

makes 9 slices

dairy-free margarine,
for greasing

6 eggs, separated

200 g/7 oz caster sugar

grated rind of 3 oranges

150 g/5½ oz
ground almonds

topping

juice of 3 oranges

3 tbsp clear honey

Preheat the oven to 180°C/350°F/Gas Mark 4. Grease a 20-cm/8-inch square cake tin and line the base. Beat the egg yolks with the sugar, orange rind and almonds in a large mixing bowl.

Whisk the egg whites in a separate large bowl until they form stiff peaks. Fold a spoonful of the egg whites into the almond mixture, then fold in the remainder. Carefully pour the mixture into the prepared cake tin.

Bake in the preheated oven for 45–50 minutes, or until a skewer inserted into the centre of the cake comes out clean. Leave to cool in the tin.

To make the topping, put the orange juice and honey into a small saucepan and bring to the boil, stir once, then cook, without stirring, for 6–8 minutes, or until reduced, thickened and syrupy. Using a fork, pierce the cake all over, then pour the syrup over the top and leave to soak in before serving.

Energy (kcals): 282   Fat (of which saturated fat): 14 g (2 g)   Carbohydrate (of which sugar): 30 g (30 g)   Salt: 0.2 g

choux buns

serves 4

115 g/4 oz gluten- and
wheat-free plain white
flour blend

½ tsp xanthan gum

55 g/2 oz dairy-free
sunflower spread, plus
extra for greasing

200 ml/7 fl oz water

2 eggs, beaten

250 g/9 oz tofu-based
cream cheese substitute

½ tsp vanilla extract

compote

350 g/12 oz summer
berries, e.g. raspberries,
redcurrants, cherries

40 g/1½ oz caster sugar

seeds from 1 vanilla pod

Preheat the oven to 220°C/425°F/Gas Mark 7. Grease two baking sheets.

Sieve together the flour and xanthan gum. Melt the spread with the water and bring to the boil. Remove from the heat and quickly beat in all the flour mixture. Cool for 1 minute. Gradually beat in the eggs with an electric whisk to make a thick, glossy dough.

Fit a 1-cm/½-inch plain piping nozzle in a piping bag and pipe about 16 golf-ball sized balls of dough onto the prepared baking sheets.

Bake in the preheated oven for 20–25 minutes, or until risen and golden brown. Cut a slit in each bun to allow steam to escape and return to the oven for 1 minute. Leave to cool on a wire rack.

Mix the tofu cheese with the vanilla and pipe into the cooled buns. For the compote, place the fruit, sugar and vanilla in a pan and heat gently until the sugar dissolves and the fruit juice runs. Spoon over the buns to serve.

Energy (kcals): 460   Fat (of which saturated fat): 34 g (8 g)   Carbohydrate (of which sugar): 30 g (8 g)   Salt: 1 g

chocolate cake

serves 8

100 g/3½ oz dairy-free
spread, plus extra
for greasing

100 g/3½ oz caster sugar

2 eggs, lightly beaten

100 g/3½ oz gluten-free
plain flour

1 tsp gluten-free
baking powder

2 tbsp cocoa powder

finely pared strips of
orange rind, to decorate

mousse

200 g/7 oz good-quality
plain dark chocolate
(about 70 per cent
cocoa solids)

grated rind of 2 oranges
and juice of 1

4 eggs, separated

Preheat the oven to 180°C/350°F/Gas Mark 4. Grease a 23-cm/9-inch round, loose-bottomed cake tin and line the base.

Cream the sugar and spread together in a mixing bowl until pale and fluffy. Gradually add the eggs, beating well with a wooden spoon between each addition. Sift the flour, baking powder and cocoa powder together, fold half into the egg mixture, then fold in the remainder. Spoon the mixture into the prepared tin and level the surface with the back of a spoon. Bake in the preheated oven for 20 minutes until risen and firm to the touch. Leave in the tin to cool completely.

Meanwhile, melt the chocolate in a heatproof bowl placed over a saucepan of gently simmering water, making sure that the bottom of the bowl does not touch the water. Leave to cool, then stir in the orange rind and juice and the egg yolks.

Whisk the egg whites in a large bowl until they form stiff peaks. Gently fold a large spoonful of the egg whites into the chocolate mixture, then fold in the remainder. Spoon the mixture on top of the cooked, cooled sponge and level the top with the back of a spoon. Alternatively, remove the sponge from the tin, slice through and sandwich with the mousse. Place in the refrigerator to set. Remove the sides of the tin if not removed earlier (though not the base) before decorating with orange rind and serving.

Energy (kcals): 407   Fat (of which saturated fat): 24 g (8.5 g)   Carbohydrate (of which sugar): 39 g (29 g)   Salt: 0.7 g

panna cotta

serves 4

4 leaves gelatine

100 ml/3½ fl oz almond milk

400 ml/14 fl oz canned coconut milk

1 stalk lemon grass, bruised

strip of lime zest

55 g/2 oz acacia honey, plus 1 tbsp

1 small pineapple

1 tbsp finely grated ginger

½ tsp ground cinnamon

juice of 1 lime

long-shred coconut, toasted, to decorate

Place the gelatine in a wide dish and pour over the almond milk. Leave to stand for 10 minutes.

Place the coconut milk, lemon grass and lime zest in a pan and heat gently, without boiling, for about 10 minutes. Add the gelatine mixture and the honey and stir on a low heat until thoroughly dissolved.

Strain the mixture into four 200-ml/7-fl oz dishes or moulds. Leave in the refrigerator until set.

Peel, core and thinly slice the pineapple. Sprinkle over the ginger, cinnamon, lime juice and 1 tablespoon of honey, turning to coat evenly. Cover and leave to stand for at least 1 hour.

To serve, quickly dip the moulds into hot water and turn out onto serving plates. Serve with the spiced pineapple, with the juices spooned over. Sprinkle with shreds of long-shred coconut to decorate.

Energy (kcals): 275   Fat (of which saturated fat): 17.5 g (15 g)   Carbohydrate (of which sugar): 27 g (24 g)   Salt: Trace

apricot cookies

makes about 16

85 g/3 oz dairy-free sunflower spread, plus extra for greasing

85 g/3 oz light muscovado sugar

1 egg, beaten

½ tsp grated nutmeg

1 tsp vanilla extract

200 g/7 oz gluten-free and wheat-free self-raising flour blend

175 g/6 oz ready-to-eat dried apricots, roughly chopped

85 g/3 oz pecan nuts, roughly chopped

Preheat the oven to 200°C/400°F/Gas Mark 6. Grease two baking sheets.

Place the spread, sugar, egg, nutmeg and vanilla in a bowl and beat until smooth. Stir in the flour, apricots and pecans, mixing to form a soft dough.

Use a tablespoon to place heaps of dough on the baking sheets, pressing with a fork to flatten slightly.

Bake the cookies for 12–15 minutes, or until golden brown. Transfer to a wire rack to cool.

Energy (kcals): 165   Fat (of which saturated fat): 9 g (1.5 g)   Carbohydrate (of which sugar): 18.5 g (10 g)   Salt: 0.2 g

strawberry roulade

serves 6

sunflower oil, for greasing

3 large eggs

125 g/4½ oz caster sugar, plus extra to sprinkle

½ tsp almond extract

55 g/2 oz gluten-free cornflour

70 g/2½ oz ground almonds

icing sugar, to decorate

filling

225 g/8 oz vegan cream cheese

1 tbsp icing sugar

200 g/7 oz strawberries, sliced

Preheat the oven to 180°C/350°F/Gas Mark 4. Grease a 20 x 30-cm/8 x 12-inch Swiss roll tin and line with non-stick baking paper.

Place the eggs, sugar and almond extract in a large bowl over a pan of hot, not boiling, water and whisk for about 10 minutes, until thick enough to hold a trail when the whisk is lifted.

Remove from the heat and whisk in the cornflour, then fold in the ground almonds lightly and evenly.

Spread the mixture into the tin and bake for 12–15 minutes, until just firm and lightly browned.

Place a sheet of baking paper on the worktop and sprinkle with caster sugar. Invert the tin over the paper to turn out the sponge. Remove the lining paper and trim the edges from the sponge. Cover with a clean tea towel and leave to cool.

To make the filling, beat together the cream cheese and icing sugar and spread over the sponge. Top with sliced strawberries and carefully roll up from one short edge.

Place on a serving plate with the join underneath, and sprinkle with icing sugar to serve.

Energy (kcals): 371   Fat (of which saturated fat): 21.5 g (4 g)   Carbohydrate (of which sugar): 37 g (29 g)   Salt: 0.5 g

banana muffins

makes 12

150 g/5½ oz gluten-free plain flour

1 tsp gluten-free baking powder

pinch of salt

150 g/5½ oz caster sugar

6 tbsp dairy-free milk

2 eggs, lightly beaten

150 g/5½ oz dairy-free spread, melted

2 small bananas, mashed

frosting

50 g/1¾ oz vegan cream cheese

2 tbsp dairy-free spread

¼ tsp ground cinnamon

90 g/3¼ oz icing sugar

Preheat the oven to 200°C/400°F/Gas Mark 6. Place 12 large paper cases in a deep muffin tin. Sift the flour, baking powder and salt together into a mixing bowl. Stir in the sugar.

Whisk the milk, eggs and spread together in a separate bowl until combined. Slowly stir into the flour mixture without beating. Fold in the mashed bananas.

Spoon the mixture into the paper cases and bake in the preheated oven for 20 minutes until risen and golden. Turn out onto a wire rack and leave to cool.

To make the frosting, beat the cream cheese and spread together in a bowl, then beat in the cinnamon and icing sugar until smooth and creamy. Chill the frosting in the refrigerator for about 15 minutes to firm up, then top each muffin with a spoonful.

Energy (kcals): 287   Fat (of which saturated fat): 16 g (4.5 g)   Carbohydrate (of which sugar): 33 g (24 g)   Salt: 0.7 g

apple galettes

*serves 4
galettes*

85 g/3 oz dairy-free sunflower spread, plus extra for greasing

55 g/2 oz golden caster sugar

85 g/3 oz hazelnuts, toasted and skinned

115 g/4 oz gluten-free and wheat-free plain flour blend, plus extra for dusting

1 egg yolk

toffee apples

3 crisp dessert apples, e.g. Cox's

55 g/2 oz sunflower spread

55 g/2 oz Demerara sugar

chopped toasted hazelnuts, to decorate

Preheat the oven to 200°C/400°F/Gas Mark 6. Grease a large baking sheet.

Place the sunflower spread, sugar, hazelnuts, flour and egg yolk in a bowl and mix well to bind to a soft dough.

Roll out the dough on a lightly floured surface to about 5 mm/¼ inch and use a 7-cm/2¾-inch cutter to cut 12 rounds. Lift onto the baking sheet and bake for 10–12 minutes or until golden. Cool for 2 minutes, then finish cooling on a wire rack.

Peel, core and slice the apples. Melt the spread in a heavy-based pan with the apples and sugar, stirring on a high heat until golden brown.

Stack the biscuits in threes with apple between each layer, spooning over the toffee. Sprinkle with chopped hazelnuts and serve warm.

Energy (kcals): 699   Fat (of which saturated fat): 45 g (8 g)   Carbohydrate (of which sugar): 70 g (47 g)   Salt: 0.7 g

mango cheesecake

serves 8

70 g/2½ oz dairy-free spread, plus extra for greasing

175 g/6 oz gluten-free and dairy-free biscuits, such as digestives, crushed

40 g/1½ oz ground almonds

filling

1 large mango, stoned, peeled and diced

juice of 1 lemon

200 g/7 oz natural soya yogurt

1 tbsp gluten-free cornflour

3 tbsp maple syrup

450 g/1 lb vegan cream cheese

topping

3 tbsp maple syrup

1 small mango, stoned, peeled and sliced

Preheat the oven to 180°C/350°F/Gas Mark 4. Lightly grease a 23-cm/9-inch round, loose-bottomed cake tin. To make the biscuit base, melt the spread in a medium-sized saucepan, then stir in the crushed biscuits and almonds. Press the mixture into the base of the prepared cake tin to make an even layer. Bake in the preheated oven for 10 minutes.

Meanwhile, to make the filling, put the mango, lemon juice, yogurt, cornflour, maple syrup and cream cheese into a food processor or blender and process until smooth and creamy. Pour the mixture over the biscuit base and smooth with the back of a spoon. Bake for 25–30 minutes, or until golden and set. Leave to cool in the tin, then transfer to a wire rack and chill in the refrigerator for 30 minutes to firm up.

To make the topping, heat the maple syrup in a frying pan. Brush the top of the cheesecake with the maple syrup. Add the mango to the remaining maple syrup in the pan and cook for 1 minute, stirring. Leave to cool slightly, then arrange the mango slices on top of the cheesecake. Pour over any remaining syrup before serving.

Energy (kcals): 429   Fat (of which saturated fat): 31 g (8 g)   Carbohydrate (of which sugar): 32 g (18 g)   Salt: 1 g

tapioca figs

serves 6

15 g/½ oz dairy-free sunflower spread, plus extra for greasing

200 g/7 oz small pearl tapioca

500 ml/18 fl oz rice milk

70 g/2½ oz golden caster sugar

seeds from 2 cardamom pods, lightly crushed

1 bay leaf

½ tsp orange flower water

6 fresh figs

pomegranate syrup, for drizzling

Grease an 18-cm/7-inch square cake tin. Place the tapioca and rice milk in a saucepan and bring to the boil. Reduce the heat and stir in the sugar, cardamom, bay leaf and the spread.

Cover and cook gently, stirring often, for 20–25 minutes or until the grains are tender.

Remove the bay leaf, stir in the orange flower water then spread into the tin and leave to cool. Chill in the refrigerator until set.

To serve, turn out the tapioca and cut into diamond shapes. Quarter the figs and arrange on plates with the tapioca shapes. Drizzle with pomegranate syrup and serve.

Energy (kcals): 327   Fat (of which saturated fat): 4 g (0.5 g)   Carbohydrate (of which sugar): 67 g (22 g)   Salt: Trace

pear granita

serves 6

75 g/2¾ oz caster sugar

1 tbsp clear honey

250 ml/9 fl oz water

225 g/8 oz just-ripe pears,
peeled, cored and sliced

2 tsp finely chopped
fresh ginger

3 tbsp lemon juice

Put the sugar, honey and water into a saucepan over a medium heat and heat, stirring, until the sugar has dissolved. Add the pears and ginger and simmer for 5 minutes, then add the lemon juice.

Tip the pears and cooking liquid into a food processor or blender and process until almost smooth. Carefully pour the mixture into a freezerproof container with a lid and leave to cool.

Put in the freezer for 2 hours until the edges and bottom of the pear mixture are frozen. Remove the container from the freezer and mix with a fork so that the frozen part of the mixture is blended with the unfrozen part. Replace the lid and return to the freezer for a further 1½ hours.

Repeat the mixing process and freeze for a further hour until the mixture forms ice crystals. Serve at this stage or return to the freezer until required, then remove 30 minutes before serving and mix again with a fork.
Serve spooned into glasses.

Energy (kcals): 113   Fat (of which saturated fat): 0.1 g (0 g)   Carbohydrate (of which sugar): 28 g (28 g)   Salt: Trace

apple crumble

serves 4

4 apples, peeled, cored and diced

5 plums, halved, stoned and quartered

4 tbsp fresh apple juice

25 g/1 oz soft light brown sugar

topping

115 g/4 oz gluten-free flour

75 g/2¾ oz dairy-free spread, diced

25 g/1 oz buckwheat flakes

25 g/1 oz rice flakes

25 g/1 oz sunflower seeds

50 g/1¾ oz soft light brown sugar

¼ tsp ground cinnamon

Preheat the oven to 180°C/350°F/Gas Mark 4. Mix the apples, plums, apple juice and sugar together in a 23-cm/9-inch round pie dish.

To make the topping, sift the flour into a mixing bowl and rub in the spread with your fingertips until it resembles coarse breadcrumbs. Stir in the buckwheat and rice flakes, sunflower seeds, sugar and cinnamon, then spoon the topping over the fruit in the dish.

Bake the crumble in the preheated oven for 30–35 minutes, or until the topping is lightly browned and crisp.

Energy (kcals): 484   Fat (of which saturated fat): 19 g (4 g)   Carbohydrate (of which sugar): 73 g (42 g)   Salt: 0.6 g

raspberry bake

serves 6

1 tbsp sunflower oil

100 g/3½ oz gluten-free and wheat-free white self-raising flour blend

2 tbsp vanilla sugar

2 eggs, beaten

250 ml/9 fl oz sweetened soya milk

175 g/6 oz raspberries

3 nectarines, halved, stoned and roughly chopped

icing sugar, for sprinkling

Preheat the oven to 220°C/425°F/Gas Mark 7. Grease a 1.7-litre/3-pint shallow metal baking dish or tin with the oil.

Place the flour, sugar, eggs and milk in a bowl and whisk to a smooth, bubbly batter. Add the raspberries.

Place the dish in the oven for 5 minutes until very hot. Add the nectarines and heat for a further minute. Remove from the oven and quickly pour in the batter and raspberries.

Bake for 25–30 minutes, until just set, risen and golden brown. Sprinkle with icing sugar and serve warm.

Energy (kcals): 147   Fat (of which saturated fat): 3 g (0.5 g)   Carbohydrate (of which sugar): 26 g (14 g)   Salt: 0.2 g

tomato focaccia

makes 1 loaf (serves 10)

3 tbsp olive oil, plus extra
for brushing

200 g/7 oz buckwheat flour

200 g/7 oz potato flour

200 g/7 oz rice flour

2 tsp xanthan gum

7 g/⅓ oz sachet gluten-free
fast-action yeast

1½ tsp salt

½ tsp black onion seeds

40 g/1½ oz sun-dried
tomatoes, soaked,
drained and chopped

600 ml/1 pint tepid water

1 small egg, beaten

2 garlic cloves,
cut into slivers

1 few sprigs fresh oregano

Brush a 33 x 23-cm/13 x 9-inch baking sheet with oil. Mix the flours, xanthan gum, yeast, salt and onion seeds in a bowl and stir in the tomatoes.

Make a well in the centre and stir in the water, egg and 1 tablespoon of oil to make a very soft dough. Beat the dough hard using a wooden spoon for 4–5 minutes, then spoon into the tin, spreading evenly with a palette knife.

Cover with oiled cling film and leave in a warm place for about 1 hour, or until doubled in size. Preheat the oven to 220°C/425°F/Gas Mark 7.

Press pieces of garlic and oregano into the dough at intervals. Drizzle with the remaining oil, then bake in the oven for 25–30 minutes, or until firm and golden brown. Turn out and cool on a wire rack.

Energy (kcals): 229   Fat (of which saturated fat): 7 g (1 g)   Carbohydrate (of which sugar): 39 g (1 g)   Salt: 1 g

pepper cornbread

makes 1 loaf (serves 10)

3 tbsp olive oil, plus extra for oiling

1 large red pepper, deseeded and sliced

175 g/6 oz fine cornmeal or polenta

115 g/4 oz gluten-free strong white flour

1 tbsp gluten-free baking powder

1 tsp salt

2 tsp sugar

250 ml/9 fl oz dairy-free milk

2 eggs, lightly beaten

Preheat the oven to 200°C/400°F/Gas Mark 6. Lightly oil a 450-g/1-lb loaf tin. Arrange the red pepper slices on a baking tray and roast in the preheated oven for 35 minutes until tender and the skin begins to blister. Set aside to cool slightly, then peel away the skin.

Meanwhile, mix the cornmeal, flour, baking powder, salt and sugar together in a large mixing bowl. Beat the milk, eggs and oil together in a separate bowl or jug and gradually add to the flour mixture. Beat with a wooden spoon to make a thick, smooth, batter-like consistency.

Finely chop the red pepper and fold into the cornmeal mixture, then spoon into the prepared tin. Bake in the preheated oven for 30 minutes until lightly golden. Leave in the tin for 10 minutes, then run a knife around the edge of the tin and turn the loaf out onto a wire rack to cool. To keep fresh, wrap the loaf in foil or seal in a polythene bag.

Energy (kcals): 180   Fat (of which saturated fat): 7 g (1.1 g)   Carbohydrate (of which sugar): 23 g (2.5 g)   Salt: 1 g

christmas puddings

serves 6

70 g/2½ oz dairy-free
sunflower spread, plus
extra for greasing

200 g/7 oz mixed dried fruit

100 ml/3½ fl oz apple juice

55 g/2 oz gluten- and
wheat-free plain white
flour blend

1 tsp ground mixed spice

30 g/1 oz breadcrumbs
from a gluten-free loaf

70 g/2½ oz dark
muscovado sugar

1 dessert apple, grated

15 g/½ oz blanched
almonds, chopped

finely grated rind 1 lemon

1 egg, beaten

sauce

200 g/7 oz vegan cream
cheese

finely grated rind ½ orange,
plus extra to decorate

1 tbsp brandy (optional)

Grease six 150-ml/5-fl oz dariole or pudding moulds and line the base of each with a round of baking paper. Soak the fruit in the apple juice for about 1 hour.

Place all the pudding ingredients in a large bowl and mix thoroughly. Pack firmly into the moulds.

Cover the puddings with a double layer of foil, twisting over at the edges to seal. Half-fill a steamer with water and bring to the boil. Steam the puddings for 50 minutes or until firm, topping up the water if necessary.

For the sauce, mix together all the ingredients until smooth. Turn out the puddings and serve with the sauce decorated with orange rind.

If not serving immediately, remove foil and cool, cover with clean foil and store in the refrigerator for up to 2 weeks. Reheat in a steamer for 15 minutes.

Energy (kcals): 410   Fat (of which saturated fat): 23 g (5 g)   Carbohydrate (of which sugar): 48 g (38 g)   Salt: 0.8 g

apples
  apple crumble 150
  apple galettes 142
  apple granola 12
  fruit soda bread 42
apricots
  apricot cookies 136
  aubergine tagine 112
  fruit soda bread 42
  millet porridge 14
artichokes: seafood pizza 72
aubergines
  aubergine tagine 112
  baba ghanoush 74
avocados
  chicken tacos 66
  chive cornbread 36
  sushi rolls 70

baba ghanoush 74
bacon/pancetta
  chive cornbread 36
  pear salad 60
bananas
  banana crêpes 10
  banana muffins 140
  banana smoothie 20
beef
  beef stew 96
  meatball pasta 98
berries
  berry crunch 16
  blueberry bars 24
  choux buns 130
  fruit soda bread 42
  raspberry bake 152
  strawberry roulade 138
  strawberry shake 22
blueberry bars 24
broccoli
  broccoli hash 38
  vegetable tempura 76
buckwheat/buckwheat flakes
  apple crumble 150
  apple granola 12
  berry crunch 16
  golden pilaf 52

carrots
  beef stew 96
  breakfast muffins 44
  golden pilaf 52
  spicy carrot soup 62
  tofu salad 64
  vegetable curry 118
  vegetable tempura 76
chicken
  chicken curry 104
  chicken tacos 66
  roast chicken 106

chickpeas
  aubergine tagine 112
  chickpea fritters 30
  lamb koftas 100
  spicy falafels 78
chive cornbread 36
chocolate
  chocolate cake 132
  mocha brownies 126
christmas pudding 158
coconut
  chicken curry 104
  coconut macaroons 124
  panna cotta 134
  prawn noodles 92
  risotto cakes 54
coeliac disease 6
cornmeal/polenta
  aubergine tagine 112
  bruschettas 56
  chive cornbread 36
  pepper cornbread 156
courgettes
  courgette quiche 82
  vegetable röstis 120
cream cheese
  banana muffins 140
  haddock flan 88
  mango cheesecake 144
  strawberry roulade 138

dairy allergies and intolerances 6
dairy-free alternatives 7
dates: apple granola 12

eggs
  broccoli hash 38
  mushroom röstis 34
  sausage brunch 32
  spanish tortilla 116

fennel
  vegetable pho 40
  vegetable röstis 120
fish & seafood
  baked lemon cod 90
  haddock flan 88
  prawn noodles 92
  salmon fingers 94
  seafood pizza 72
  spicy sea bass 114
  sushi rolls 70
food allergies and intolerances 6

gluten allergies and
  intolerances 6
gluten-free alternatives 7

haddock flan 88

lamb koftas 100
lentils: spicy carrot soup 62

mango cheesecake 144
millet flakes
  apple granola 12
  berry crunch 16
  millet porridge 14
mushrooms
  aubergine tagine 112
  mushroom pasta 86
  mushroom röstis 34
  pork pies 102
  vegetable pho 40
  vegetable tempura 76

noodles
  prawn noodles 92
  spring rolls 68
  tofu salad 64
  vegetable pho 40
nuts
  apple galettes 142
  apple granola 12
  apricot cookies 136
  banana smoothie 20
  beef stew 96
  blueberry bars 24
  coconut macaroons 124
  mango cheesecake 144
  mocha brownies 126
  orange cake 128
  peachy tofu fool 18
  pear salad 60
  strawberry roulade 138
  strawberry shake 22

onion soup 50
oranges
  breakfast muffins 44
  chocolate cake 132
  orange cake 128

panna cotta 134
pasta
  meatball pasta 98
  mushroom pasta 86
peachy tofu fool 18
pears
  pear granita 148
  pear salad 60
peppers
  broccoli hash 38
  chicken tacos 66
  pepper cornbread 156
  prawn noodles 92
  vegetable röstis 120
plums
  apple crumble 150
  plum pancakes 26
pork
  pork pies 102
  spring rolls 68

potatoes
  basil gnocchi 80
  broccoli hash 38
  pork pies 102
  potato cakes 28
  potato salad 48
  salmon fingers 94
  sausage brunch 32
  spanish tortilla 116
  vegetable curry 118
  vegetable röstis 120
prunes: fruit soda bread 42

quinoa/quinoa flakes
  blueberry bars 24
  tabbouleh 58

raspberry bake 152
rice
  risotto cakes 54
  squash risotto 108
  sushi rolls 70
rice flakes
  apple crumble 150
  apple granola 12
  berry crunch 16

sausage brunch 32
spinach
  mushroom pasta 86
  risotto cakes 54
  vegetable curry 118
spring rolls 68
squash risotto 108
strawberry roulade 138
strawberry shake 22
sushi rolls 70

tabbouleh 58
tapioca figs 146
tofu
  peachy tofu fool 18
  thai tofu cakes 110
  tofu salad 64
  vegetable tempura 76
tomatoes
  aubergine tagine 112
  basil gnocchi 80
  bruschettas 56
  chicken curry 104
  courgette quiche 82
  meatball pasta 98
  potato salad 48
  roast chicken 106
  sausage brunch 32
  seafood pizza 72
  tabbouleh 58
  tomato focaccia 154
  vegetable curry 118
  vegetable röstis 120

wheat allergies and
  intolerances 6
wheat-free alternatives 7